SISTER L

and Other Crime

Marcia lives with her father and her sister, Karin. She does not have a job. Her father is ill and needs someone with him all the time. So Marcia stays at home. It is not an easy life, and Karin does not help. Is it a crime to hate your sister?

Joey does not have a sister, and he does not have a job. So how does he live, where does he get his money from? From crime. Small crimes at first, but they get bigger, and bigger. Joey doesn't call it crime, he calls it luck – Joey's luck. But everybody knows that luck does not last for ever . . .

Rosa has a job, but she does not make much money. So on Monday evenings she does something different – she asks people for 'hush money'. In other words, she sells her silence. But silence about what? And who is worse, the person who sells the silence, or the person who buys the silence?

Three different crimes, three different criminals . . .

OXFORD BOOKWORMS LIBRARY
Crime & Mystery

Sister Love
and Other Crime Stories
Stage 1 (400 headwords)

Series Editor: Jennifer Bassett
Founder Editor: Tricia Hedge
Activities Editors: Jennifer Bassett and Christine Lindop

JOHN ESCOTT

Sister Love

and Other Crime Stories

Illustrated by
Gavin Reece

OXFORD UNIVERSITY PRESS

OXFORD

UNIVERSITY PRESS

Great Clarendon Street, Oxford OX2 6DP

Oxford University Press is a department of the University of Oxford.
It furthers the University's objective of excellence in research, scholarship,
and education by publishing worldwide in

Oxford New York

Auckland Cape Town Dar es Salaam Hong Kong Karachi
Kuala Lumpur Madrid Melbourne Mexico City Nairobi
New Delhi Shanghai Taipei Toronto

With offices in

Argentina Austria Brazil Chile Czech Republic France Greece
Guatemala Hungary Italy Japan Poland Portugal Singapore
South Korea Switzerland Thailand Turkey Ukraine Vietnam

OXFORD and OXFORD ENGLISH are registered trade marks of
Oxford University Press in the UK and in certain other countries

ISBN 978 0 19 478921 9

A complete recording of this Bookworms edition of
Sister Love and Other Crime Stories is available on audio CD ISBN 978 0 19 478856 4

Printed in China

Word count (main text): 5565 words

For more information on the Oxford Bookworms Library,
visit www.oup.com/bookworms

CONTENTS

Sister Love

Marcia met Howard Collins at church. Marcia was thirty-five years old, Howard was forty-one. Howard lived with his mother in a small house on the south side of the town. Marcia lived with her sister and father in an apartment, three streets away.

Marcia did not work. Her father, George Grant, was ill and never left the apartment. He stayed in bed most of the time and always needed somebody with him. So Marcia stayed at home with her father, and only went out when her sister Karin was in the house.

The two sisters were very different. Marcia was short with a small round face and short black hair. Karin was ten years younger. She was tall, had long brown hair, and good legs, and a suntan all through the summer. People often said to Marcia, 'Your sister is very beautiful.' There were always lots of men ready to take Karin out to dinner or to the cinema. But Marcia stayed at home.

Karin worked in a shop in the town. When she was at home, she liked to sit up on the roof garden of their apartment building.

It was one Sunday in May when Marcia came home with Howard the first time. She took him to see her father. George Grant was in bed. He had grey hair and a grey face. Sometimes he read a book, but mostly he just sat in bed and watched television.

'This is Howard, father,' Marcia said. 'He works at the hospital, and we met at church. I told you about him last week. Do you remember?'

'No,' her father said. And he turned his face away, back to his television. He was not interested in new people or his daughters' friends.

Just then, Karin came into the room. She wore a white bikini and white shoes. She smiled at Howard.

'So you're Howard,' she said. 'My big sister has got a boyfriend at last!'

Howard's face went red and he looked down at his feet.

Karin laughed. 'Come on up to the roof garden and have some wine. The sun is wonderful this morning.'

'Oh, I . . .' Howard began.

Marcia looked angrily at her sister. But then she said, 'Yes, I must get father a drink. See you in a minute, Howard. Go up to the roof and talk to Karin.'

The sun was hot on the roof and Howard took off his coat. He looked around. There were three chairs, a sun umbrella, a sunbed, and a table with three glasses and a bottle of wine on it. There were tiles on the floor, and next to the little wall around the edge of the roof there were some flowers in boxes. This was the 'garden'.

'Very nice,' said Howard.

Karin smiled at him.

Howard looked around. 'Very nice,' he said.

'We don't see many good-looking men up here,' she said. 'Sit down and have a drink.'

Howard's face went red again. He gave a shy little laugh. 'Oh, er . . . thank you,' he said. He tried not to look at Karin's long suntanned legs, but it was not easy.

'I come up here all the time when it's sunny,' Karin said. She began to put suntan oil on her arms and legs. Howard watched.

Then Marcia arrived, and the three of them sat in the sun and drank wine. Marcia looked at Howard with love in her eyes. She did not look at Karin.

Karin watched them. Her eyes went from her sister, to Howard, and back again to her sister. She smiled.

It was not a nice smile.

❊ ❊ ❊

Every Sunday morning after that, Marcia brought Howard home for a glass of wine after church. Howard stopped his car in the street outside the apartment building, and Marcia said, 'Sound the horn, Howard. Tell Karin we're here, then she can get the wine ready.'

So Howard gave three little toots on his car horn. On sunny days Karin always came to the wall at the edge of the roof, and looked over to wave at them. Then she went to get the wine.

She always wore her bikini or a very short skirt. Marcia never wore short skirts or a bikini.

4

On sunny days Karin always came to the wall at the edge of the roof, and looked over to wave at them.

'My legs are too fat for bikinis,' she told Howard.

'Your legs are . . . very nice,' he said shyly.

One day in June Karin asked Howard, 'What time do you finish work, Howard?'

'About six o'clock,' he said.

'Could you bring me home after work?' Karin said. 'My shop's very near the hospital – you drive right past it. And you only live three streets away from us.'

'There's a very good bus,' said Marcia quickly. 'It stops outside our building.'

'But the bus is so slow!' Karin said. 'Please, Howard!'

'Please, Howard!' said Karin.

Howard looked from one sister to the other. 'Oh, well . . . er, yes, all right then,' he said.

'Thank you!' Karin said, and gave him a quick kiss.

So every evening Howard drove Karin home. On the first Friday they were an hour late. When they arrived, Marcia was at the door of the apartment building.

'What happened?' she asked. 'Why are you so late?'

'There was an accident,' Karin said. 'Three cars, all across the road – on that hill by the cinema, you know. We couldn't get past, we couldn't go back. There were so many cars! Nobody could move!'

Howard said nothing.

※　　※　　※

It was a long, hot summer that year. Marcia went to church every Sunday morning, and Karin stayed at home with their father. When it was sunny – and it often was – Karin went up to her sunbed on the roof.

When Marcia went up to the roof garden, she always sat under the umbrella. But Karin put on lots of suntan oil and sat in the sun in her bikini.

'The hot sun's not good for your body,' Marcia said.

Karin laughed. 'Howard likes my body.'

'No, he doesn't!' Marcia said angrily.

'Oh, he does!' Karin said. 'He's very shy with women, but he always looks at my body *very* carefully. He does it all the time. Perhaps he wants me to take off—'

7

'Stop it, Karin!' Marcia said. 'Don't say those things!'

Karin laughed. 'What's the matter, big sister? Are you afraid I'm going to take him from you?'

Marcia did not answer.

※　※　※

The next Sunday, Howard phoned Marcia early in the morning.

'I – I don't feel very well,' he said. 'I'm not going to church today.'

'My love, I'm sorry,' Marcia said. 'Can I phone you when I get home?'

'Yes, of course,' he said.

'I can't phone before one o'clock,' Marcia said. 'I'm going to be late back because there's a meeting after church. Something about Africa, I think.'

'Oh yes, I remember,' Howard said.

But Marcia was wrong. There was no meeting after church that morning. It was the next Sunday. So she left church at the usual time and arrived home at a quarter to twelve.

First she went in to see her father, but he was asleep. Then she phoned Howard, but there was no answer.

'Perhaps he's sleeping,' she thought. 'And his mother doesn't want to answer the phone.'

She went to her room and put on a long summer skirt. Then she went up to the roof garden.

She put her hand on the door to the roof . . . and stopped. The door was half open and she could hear voices. There was someone with Karin.

A man. Howard. *Howard?*

Marcia listened.

Marcia could hear voices.

'I feel bad about this,' Howard said. 'We must tell Marcia soon, Karin.'

'No!' Karin said quickly. She gave a little laugh. 'It's our secret, Howard. Only for a little longer. All right?'

'I – I don't like . . .' he began.

'But you do love *me*, Howard,' Karin said. 'Not Marcia? Say you love me. Please!'

Marcia suddenly felt cold.

'You . . . you know I do,' Howard answered. 'But—'

Karin kissed him. 'It's our little secret. Oh, is your car outside, my love? We don't want Marcia to see it.'

'I didn't bring my car,' Howard said. 'I walked here.'

'Good,' Karin said. 'But it's getting late. You must go, before she comes home.'

They kissed again.

'See you tomorrow, usual time, usual place,' said Karin. 'Now, go!'

Marcia moved quickly and quietly away from the roof door, and ran to her bedroom. She did not want Howard or Karin to see her.

She heard their voices. Then the front door of the apartment opened and closed. Howard was gone.

Marcia sat on her bed for an hour. 'Why, why, *why*?' she thought. '*Why* does she do it? I stay at home with an old man all the time. I can't go out to work, I can't make new friends, I can't meet new people. I go shopping once

10

a week and I go to church once a week. That's all. And then I met Howard. When he said "I love you", I was so happy. And now . . . ?'

Karin had everything. Good looks, a job, friends. She was young, she was beautiful, she could have any man. So why Howard? Why, why, *why*?

'It's not because she wants *him*,' Marcia thought. 'It's because *I* love him. It's because she doesn't want *me* to be happy.'

But you do love me, Howard. Not Marcia?

You know I do.

Was it true? Did Howard love Karin and not her? No! He saw only the beautiful, suntanned body. He didn't *know* her.

'She's not going to have him . . .' Marcia thought.

✷   ✷   ✷

Every evening that week, Howard drove Karin home after work. And every evening they got later and later.

The next Sunday, Marcia didn't go to church.

'I've got a bad head,' she told Karin. 'I just phoned Howard and told him, and he's coming here after church as usual. I'm going back to sleep for an hour or two.' And she went into her bedroom and shut the door.

Later in the morning, when Karin was with their father, Marcia went up to the roof garden. Karin's bottle of suntan oil was on the table, and Marcia smiled.

When Karin came up to the roof, Marcia was in her chair under the umbrella with a book in her hand.

'Oh, is your head better?' Karin asked.

'Yes, thanks,' Marcia said.

Karin wore her bikini, a new yellow one. She opened her bottle of suntan oil.

Karin opened her bottle of suntan oil.

'Oh, there's not much here,' she said. 'I must get some more.' She began to put some oil on her legs.

Twenty minutes later, Howard stopped his car in the street below. Up on the roof, Karin and Marcia heard the usual three little toots on his car horn.

'He's here,' Karin said excitedly. 'Your man's here, big sister!' And she laughed.

Yes, Marcia thought. *My man, not yours, Karin.*

Karin jumped up from her sunbed. She ran to the wall at the edge of the roof to look down and wave to Howard. She had no shoes on, and at the wall her feet suddenly slipped away from under her.

'Aaagh!' she cried.

She fell forward, and put out her hands to grab the wall. But the top of the wall was slippery too. Her hands could not hold it, and slipped away, off the wall, over the edge. And her body went on too, over the edge of the wall, and down . . .

Down . . . down . . . down . . .

Before she hit the ground, she knew.

Slippery . . . suntan oil . . . Marcia . . .

Joey's Luck

Joey Kerrigan arrived in London in January 1912. He did not have a place to stay.

'It doesn't matter,' he thought, smiling. 'Joey's luck is going to find me a room.'

Joey thought a lot about luck. 'One day I'm going to be rich,' he told everybody. 'Lucky people get rich, and I'm lucky.'

After a lot of walking, he found a room in a house. It was near Tower Bridge. The room wasn't very big but it was cheap. The landlord's name was Mr Webber. He looked Joey up and down.

'What's your name?' he said. 'Where are you from?'

'Joe. Joe . . . Smith,' Joe said. 'I'm from Ireland.'

'Well, you can have the room,' Webber said, 'but I want two weeks' money now.'

'I've only got one week's money,' Joey said.

'And tomorrow's Sunday,' Webber said. 'You can't find work on a Sunday. So when can you give me the second week's money?'

Joey smiled with his mouth but not his eyes. 'I can find

14

work,' he said. 'I'm lucky. Good things happen to me. It's called Joey's luck.'

❀ ❀ ❀

On Sunday Joey stayed in bed all morning and in the afternoon he went for a walk. After an hour, he took a bag from a woman in Fleet Street.

Joey took a bag from a woman in Fleet Street.

The woman shouted, 'Stop! Stop!'

But Joey was now fifty metres away, and there were no other people near.

Joey laughed and ran down a little street, then between two tall buildings down to the river.

He stopped and opened the bag. There was some money in it, but not very much. He took the money out, then put the bag into the river.

Later that day, he walked past a bookshop. There were lots of people there, looking at books, and Joey moved carefully between them. For a second he stood behind a fat man, then moved quietly away. The man did not feel Joey's hand in his back pocket, but the man's wallet was now inside Joey's shirt.

Joey was a very good pickpocket.

It was a big, fat wallet, and when he got back to the house, he gave the landlord the second week's money for the room.

'You found work on a Sunday?' Webber said. 'Where? Who with?'

Joey smiled. 'I told you, I'm lucky. Joey's luck!'

❀ ❀ ❀

For the next three months, Joey Kerrigan walked the streets of London most days. He stole handbags from women, or things from shops, and he took wallets from men's pockets. One morning at the beginning of April, he took a wallet from the pocket of an old man with a red face. Joey was usually a very good pickpocket – people never knew anything about it.

But not that morning. The man with the red face was quick. He turned, saw Joey, and shouted.

'Hey! You! That's my wallet! Come back here!'

But Joey was a good runner too. In two seconds he was round the corner into another street, then round another corner, and then he jumped onto a bus.

'Joey's luck!' Joey said, laughing.

❀ ❀ ❀

There was more luck for Joey that week.

He first learned about Theo Goldman's money in a pub near his landlord's house. Webber went to the pub most evenings and sat with his friend, Goldman.

Goldman had a shop not far from the pub. He bought and sold a lot of different things – tables, chairs, beds, clocks, watches, books, pictures . . .

When Joey went into the pub that evening, he saw Webber and Goldman at a table near the window. There were a lot of people in the pub. Joey bought a drink, then found a chair near Webber and Goldman. They did not see him. Joey sat with his back to them, and listened.

'But I need money to buy things when people bring them in,' Goldman said.

'*Some* money, yes,' Webber answered. 'But a hundred pounds or more? And in the shop? No, no, Theo!'

'It's not in the shop,' Goldman said. 'It's in my room at the back.'

'Do you have a good place to put it?' Webber said.

Goldman laughed. 'A very good place,' he said.

Joey sat with his drink, thinking. He knew Goldman's shop because it was in the same street as Webber's house. Joey often walked past it.

A hundred pounds or more. 'I'm going to get that hundred pounds!' he thought. 'Then I can do anything! Perhaps begin a new life in America!'

He smiled. Joey's luck again!

So the money was in the room at the back, in *a very good place.* But where was that place?

The next morning Joey walked slowly past Goldman's shop. He did not go in, but looked through the window.

The old man was in the shop, but he did not see Joey.

Joey did not go in, but looked through the window.

Joey saw an open door to the room at the back of the shop. Through the door he could see a table, two chairs, and a big cupboard. Was Goldman's money in that cupboard?

Suddenly, the old man looked up, and Joey quickly turned and walked away.

❧ ❧ ❧

He did not go to bed that night. He put all his things into a bag, sat in an armchair and waited. Midnight came, and went. At two o'clock in the morning he went down the stairs and out of the house.

It was a cold night and Joey looked up at the moon in the sky.

'Are you a lucky moon?' he said, smiling. 'Joey's lucky moon?'

He walked to Goldman's shop and looked round. Nobody was in the street. He took a small hammer from his coat pocket and broke the glass in the shop door. Then he put his hand through and opened the door.

Joey moved quickly into the shop. He closed the door behind him and put his bag on the floor. Then he walked quietly across the shop to the door into the back room, opened it, and went through. It was dark, but moonlight came through the window, and Joey could see the big cupboard.

The little hammer soon opened the cupboard. There

The little hammer soon opened the cupboard.

were a lot of books and papers inside; some of the papers
fell out on to the floor.

'*Who's there?*'

Joey did not move. Only his eyes moved, looking
around the room. Then a door at the back of the room

opened, and Theo Goldman came in with an oil lamp. He saw Joey.

'What—!' he began.

Joey jumped across the room, grabbed the old man's arm, and pulled it up behind his back. Then he held the hammer in front of Goldman's face.

Joey pulled the old man's arm up behind his back.

'Where's the money?' he said. 'Tell me!'

'M-money?' Goldman said. 'What – what money? There isn't any money.'

'Yes, there is,' Joey said. 'You told Webber about it in the pub. A hundred pounds or more. Where is it?'

Goldman said nothing.

'Tell me,' Joey said, 'or I'm going to break your arms! First one arm, and then the other one. *Where is it?*'

Goldman tried to pull his arm away. He made small angry noises, but no words came out.

Joey held the hammer in front of Goldman's eyes. '*Tell me!* Or this hammer goes into your face!'

'All right! All right! It – it's under the floor,' Goldman said. 'Under the cupboard.'

Joey pushed the old man across to the cupboard. 'Get it,' he said. 'Now!'

The old man put the oil lamp on the floor and pulled the cupboard away from the wall. Then he got between the cupboard and the wall and pulled up some of the floor. There was a small box under the floor and Goldman got it out.

Joey grabbed the box from the old man's hands, and opened it. It was full of money.

Joey smiled.

'I know you!' Goldman said suddenly. 'You live at Albert Webber's house!'

'Albert who?' said Joey. 'Don't know him.'

He began to take the money out of the box and push it into the pockets of his coat.

'Yes, you do! You live in his house,' Goldman said. 'Albert told me about you. You're—'

'Be quiet!' Joey said. 'All right, so you know me. But nobody's going to *find* me.' He laughed. 'I can get a long way away with this money.'

All the money from Goldman's box was now in Joey's pockets. He gave Goldman a little push. 'Now, get back in your bedroom and stay there.' He pushed him again. 'Go on! Get moving!'

The old man began to walk across the room with the oil lamp. Suddenly, he turned and hit Joey on the head with the lamp.

'Aaagh!' cried Joey.

The lamp broke and fell on the floor, next to the papers from the cupboard. The oil from the lamp ran across the floor, carrying the flames to the papers.

Goldman tried to run into the shop but Joey jumped on him and the two of them fell to the floor. The old man's head hit the wall. After that, he did not move.

Joey heard the noise of the flames before he saw them. He looked behind him. The flames were big, and were already halfway up the legs of a table.

Joey jumped to his feet and ran through the shop. He

The flames were already halfway up the legs of a table.

found his bag by the front door, went out into the street and began to run again. At the end of the street, he stopped and looked back.

There were now flames in the shop window, and black smoke came from the shop door. He thought about the old man on the floor in the back room – but only for a second.

Then he turned and ran again.

♣ ♣ ♣

Two days later, on Wednesday 10th April, 1912, Joey was in Southampton, with thousands of other people. They came to see the new ship there – the biggest and fastest ship in the world. It was the day of its first voyage across the Atlantic to New York, carrying more than two thousand people.

Some of the people in Southampton that day were the ship's passengers. Some of them just came to look at the wonderful new ship.

And there it was! Joey was a happy young man. He was a passenger, with a ticket in his pocket – a ticket to New York! Life was good, he thought.

'Joey's luck got me the money for my ticket!' he said, laughing. 'And Joey's luck is taking me to America. This is the end of my old life!'

And he walked onto the *Titanic*.

Hush Money

Behind *The Green Bird* pub there was a big car park. It was a busy pub, and every night there were lots of cars there. Tonight, there was a woman in the car park too. She stood in the dark behind a tree, watching and waiting.

Her name was Rosa, and she was twenty years old. She worked in a hotel six days a week but not on Mondays. On Mondays, Rosa did something different.

And today was Monday.

It was cold. Rosa pushed her hands into the pockets of her coat. It was a night for trousers, but Rosa wore a short skirt and nothing on her legs. That was important.

After a time a woman came out of the pub and walked across the car park to a blue Ford car. The woman was about fifty years old and she walked slowly. She sang quietly, with a little smile on her face.

'She's drunk,' Rosa thought. 'But she's going to drive.'

The woman got to her car and put a hand on it. She wore a long green coat and grey trousers, and she had blonde hair. Very, very blonde hair.

'Oh dear, my head!' she said, then laughed.

'That hair colour came out of a bottle,' Rosa thought.

She took a small bottle from her pocket. There was some red liquid in it and she put some of the liquid on her leg. Then she ran quickly round the car park to the blue Ford.

Rosa ran quickly round the car park to the blue Ford.

The woman opened the car door and half-fell into the driving seat. She laughed. 'Oh, Dorothy Burns,' she sang. 'You're drunk again!'

Rosa was now behind her car, crouching on the ground. When the car began to move back, she jumped to her feet and hit the car with her hand – bang!

The car stopped suddenly and Rosa fell down on the ground behind the car. She put her hand on the red liquid on her leg, and quickly put some of it on the back of the car.

Dorothy Burns got out of her car, and walked round to the back. When she saw Rosa on the ground, her face went white.

'Oh!' she cried. 'What – what happened?'

'My leg!' Rosa said. 'Oh, my leg!' She began to cry.

'But – but what happened?' said Dorothy Burns. Then she saw the red liquid on Rosa's leg. 'Oh, there's blood on your leg!'

'Yes, because your car hit me, that's why!' Rosa said. She stopped crying, and began to look angry.

'I – I didn't see you behind me,' Dorothy Burns said.

'You didn't see me because you didn't *look*,' Rosa said angrily. She stared at the woman. 'You're drunk!'

Dorothy Burns was suddenly very afraid. 'I – I . . .'

'Yes, you smell of whisky! I can smell it from here,' Rosa said. 'I'm going to call the police. Now!'

When Dorothy saw Rosa on the ground, her face went white.

'Oh no, please!' Dorothy Burns said. 'I'm very, very sorry, but not the police, please! Listen, I can help you. I can drive you home and—'

'I'm not getting in that car with you!' Rosa said. 'You're drunk!'

31

'No!' Dorothy Burns said. 'Just one small whisky, that's all.'

'Oh yes? Tell that to the police.' Rosa stood up, holding her leg. 'What's the number of your car?'

'No! Please!' Dorothy Burns said. 'Not the police. Listen, I want to help you. Take a taxi to the hospital – I can give you the money for it. Go to the accident—'

'How much money?' said Rosa.

'Um . . . er, twenty pounds?' Dorothy Burns said.

'Fifty,' Rosa said.

'Well, how about thirty?' said Dorothy Burns.

'Fifty.'

'But I haven't got a lot of money with me.'

'Fifty. I'm calling the police now.' Rosa took a mobile phone out of her coat pocket.

'OK, OK,' said Dorothy Burns. She got her handbag from the car, took out fifty pounds, and gave the money to Rosa. 'Here you are,' she said.

Rosa took the money, and walked away. She went down the street to her car, a small, white Fiat, ten years old. She sat in the car and waited for the woman to drive away. Then Rosa drove home.

@ @ @

On the next three Monday evenings, Rosa went to three different pubs. She waited for a drunk or nearly drunk driver to come out. Sometimes she waited two hours or

more. Then she took out her little bottle of red liquid –
and minutes later there was an 'accident'.

The drivers never wanted Rosa to call the police. They
were always ready to give her money. Sometimes it was
fifty pounds, sometimes a hundred. Once, a big fat man
with gold teeth gave her two hundred pounds. That was
a very good Monday.

◎   ◎   ◎

The next Monday, Rosa found a pub in a street not far
from *The Green Bird*. It was a very cold night, so she
waited in her car. After an hour a man came out of the
pub with a bottle of wine in one hand. He stood looking
up and down the car park. Rosa watched him.

'He can't find his car,' she thought. 'He's drunk.'

After a minute or two, the man began to walk across
the car park to a big red Honda. Twice his foot slipped
and he nearly fell. But at last he got to the Honda and
began to open the door.

Rosa put some red liquid on her leg and got out of her
car. She walked quickly to the Honda and crouched
down at the back of it, ready for the 'accident'.

'Hey, you!'

Rosa quickly looked round. A woman ran across the
car park – a woman in a green coat and grey trousers, a
woman with very blonde hair. She had a camera in her
hand.

'Hey, you!'

Rosa stood up and began to walk away, but Dorothy Burns was quicker than she was.

'Oh no, you don't!' Dorothy shouted. She grabbed Rosa's arm. 'You were at *The Green Bird* four weeks ago.'

'What? Who are you? What are you talking about?' said Rosa. 'I'm just going home. Let go of my arm!'

The man with the wine bottle in his hand came round to the back of his Honda. 'Hey! What are we doing, what's happening?' he said. His face was very red and his eyes were half-closed.

'This woman took fifty pounds from me four weeks ago,' Dorothy Burns told him. 'She's a fake. She gets down behind your car – and then says your car hit her! But it doesn't! She does it to get money out of you. She says, "Oh, you're drunk, and I'm going to call the police." And because you *are* drunk and you're afraid, you give her money to stop her. I did.'

The man looked at Rosa. 'Wh-a-a-a-t?' he said.

Rosa pulled her arm away, but before she could run, Dorothy Burns grabbed her other arm.

'Look at her leg,' she said to the man. 'That's blood on it. But why? How did it get there? *She* put it there – all ready for the accident. *Your* accident. Because in a minute you're going to hit her with your car. And then she's going to cry out, "Oh, my leg! My leg". But nothing happened! She's a fake!'

At last the man understood. He stared at Rosa and his face got redder. 'You little . . .!' he said angrily. He pushed Rosa, and she fell to the ground. But before he could hit her again, Dorothy Burns pulled him away.

'No, wait,' she said.

The bottle of wine fell from the man's hand. It hit the ground next to Rosa and broke. Wine went over her face and her coat.

'My wine!' the man cried. He looked angrily at the two

The man stared at Rosa and his face got redder.

women, then began to walk back to the pub. 'Got to get some more wine,' he said. 'For my wife.'

Rosa stood up slowly and then began to walk away.

'Wait!' said Dorothy Burns.

Rosa laughed. 'Why? I don't want to talk to you.'

'Oh, I think you do,' Dorothy Burns said. 'You see, I took some photos of you – when you were behind that man's car, waiting. Interesting photos, they are.'

Rosa stopped, then walked back to Dorothy. 'How did you find me?' she said.

'I went to a different pub every night. And waited in the car parks and watched. And here you are – doing your dirty little blackmail again.'

'It's not blackmail,' said Rosa quickly. 'He *was* drunk. And *you* were drunk too, that other night.'

'But my car didn't hit you!' said Dorothy.

'How do you know?' said Rosa. 'You were drunk!'

'No, not drunk. Just happy, that's all,' said Dorothy. 'When I got home, I began to think. You wanted that fifty pounds – you wanted it very much. And I know all about blackmail. You see, I was a fake once, too.'

Rosa stared at her. 'What did you do?' she asked.

'When I was a child,' said Dorothy Burns, 'my mother and father often went out in the evenings – to dinner, to their friends, to the cinema . . . They always got a babysitter in to stay with me because I was only ten

years old. The babysitters were always girls, usually
students, about eighteen or nineteen years old. They
needed the money badly. Students always do. But I liked
money too.'

Dorothy Burns smiled. 'It was easy. At first I was nice
to them. Then I said, "I want half your babysitting
money, or I'm going to tell mummy about you. I'm going
to say things like this. You hit me. You put very hot
water on my hands. You pull my hair. You put me in the
dark . . ." These things weren't true, of course. But the
girls were afraid of my mother. She was famous, you see.
She wrote books about children, and was always on
television. And when she was angry, she wasn't a very
nice person. And so the babysitters said nothing, and
gave me half their money.'

'What a nice child you were!' Rosa said.

'No, I wasn't nice,' said Dorothy. 'But some people get
nicer when they get older. I don't do blackmail now, but
I know a blackmailer when I see one.'

She smiled at Rosa, and Rosa stared back at her.

'What do you want?' she said.

Dorothy Burns put out her hand. 'I want my fifty
pounds back, of course.'

๑ ๑ ๑

Three minutes later, Rosa drove her little Fiat out of the
pub car park. She was *very* angry.

'*I want my fifty pounds back, of course.*'

Because she was angry, she drove very fast.

Two kilometres from the pub, Rosa's car went off the road and hit a wall. She didn't die, but she broke one arm, one leg, and hit her head badly on the car. She couldn't move, she couldn't get out of the car, she couldn't get her mobile phone . . .

Two policemen found her in her car an hour later, and called an ambulance. Rosa's face was white and she couldn't speak. The policemen were not friendly.

'I can smell wine on her,' the first policeman said.

'Another drunk driver!' the second policeman said. 'Why do people drink and drive?'

GLOSSARY

apartment a group of rooms for living in (part of a larger house)

babysitter a person who looks after your child while you are away from home

bikini a piece of clothing in two pieces that women wear for swimming and lying in the sun

blackmail saying that you will tell something bad about somebody if they do not give you money

blonde (of hair) light yellow or gold in colour

blood the red liquid inside your body

buy (past tense **bought**) to get something with money

church a building where people go to pray to God

crouch *(v)* to bend your knees and back so that your body is close to the ground

drunk *(adj)* people get drunk after drinking too much alcohol

edge the part along the end or side of something

fake *(n)* a copy of something, made to trick people

fall (past tense **fell**) to go down suddenly

flame the bright red/orange parts of a fire

glass you drink water from a glass

good-looking nice to look at

grab to take something quickly and roughly

hammer a tool with a handle and a heavy metal part, used for hitting nails into wood

horn a thing in a car that makes a loud sound

jump to move quickly with both feet off the ground

kiss *(v)* to touch someone lovingly with your mouth

lamp (oil) a thing that burns oil to give light

landlord   a man who owns a house and other people pay to live
     in it
liquid   water, oil and milk are liquids
luck   chance: things (good or bad) that happen to you
marry   to take somebody as your husband or wife
moon   the big thing that shines in the sky at night
passenger   a person who travels in a bus, ship, etc.
pickpocket   a person who steals things from people's pockets
pub   a place where people go to have a drink, meet friends, etc.
roof   the top of a building
secret   something that you do not want other people to know
sell (past tense **sold**)   to give something to somebody and get
     money for it
shout   to speak very loudly
shy   not able to talk easily to people you do not know
slip *(v)*   to move on something smooth or wet and nearly fall
slippery   difficult to hold or stand on because it is smooth or wet
sound *(v)*   to make a sound
stare *(v)*   to look at somebody for a long time
steal (past tense **stole**)   to take something that is not yours
suntan   the brown colour of skin that has been in the sun
suntan oil   liquid that you put on your skin to help it to go
     brown
tile   a flat square thing that people use to cover walls and floors
toot *(n)*   a short high sound made by a car horn
turn *(v)*   to move your body round
wallet   a small flat case to carry money in
wave *(v)*   to move your hand to say hello or goodbye to someone
wear (past tense **wore**)   to have clothes on your body
wine   a drink made from grapes

Sister Love
and Other Crime Stories

ACTIVITIES

Before Reading

1 **Read the story introduction on the first page of the book, and the back cover. What do you know now about the stories? Tick one box for each sentence.**

	YES	NO
1 Karin and Marcia are good friends.	☐	☐
2 Marcia stays at home because she wants to.	☐	☐
3 Karin has a more interesting life than her sister.	☐	☐
4 Joey works hard to get his money.	☐	☐
5 In the beginning, Joey's crimes are small.	☐	☐
6 People like Joey so they give him money.	☐	☐
7 Rosa makes a lot of money in her job.	☐	☐
8 People give Rosa money because they are afraid of her.	☐	☐
9 Rosa sells her silence once a week.	☐	☐

2 **What happens in these stories? Can you guess? Choose one answer for each of these questions.**

1 At the end of *Sister Love*, one person is dead. Who is it?

a) Marcia.

b) Karin.

c) Marcia's father.

d) Marcia's boyfriend.

2 In *Sister Love*, the person dies because of a liquid.
   Which liquid is it?
   a) Very hot cooking oil.
   b) Red wine.
   c) Bath water.
   d) Suntan oil.

3 In *Joey's Luck*, what does Joey do at the end of the
   story?
   a) He leaves the country.
   b) He goes to the police.
   c) He dies in a fire.
   d) He lives a better life.

4 In *Hush Money*, Rosa meets somebody. What is this
   person like?
   a) Nicer than Rosa.
   b) Cleverer than Rosa.
   c) Very old and very rich.
   d) Very ill.

3 **Some of these things are in the stories, but not all of them.
   Can you guess which ones? Tick some boxes.**

   ☐ a gun   ☐ a car park   ☐ a bicycle   ☐ a bikini
   ☐ a pub   ☐ a photo   ☐ a suitcase   ☐ a cupboard
   ☐ a fire   ☐ a knife   ☐ a ship   ☐ a river
   ☐ a train   ☐ a ticket   ☐ a hammer   ☐ a dog
   ☐ a letter ☐ a radio   ☐ a garden   ☐ a camera

While Reading

Read *Sister Love* to the bottom of page 9. Can you guess what happens next? Choose answers to these questions.

1 What does Marcia learn?
   a) Karin is taking Howard from her.
   b) Howard wants to marry Karin.
   c) Karin and Howard are going to go away together.
   d) Howard loves Karin, but she is tired of him.
2 What is Marcia going to do?
   a) She is going to kill Howard and Karin.
   b) She is going to kill Howard.
   c) She is going to kill Karin.
   d) She is going to tell people at church about Howard.

Read *Joey's Luck*, and then put these halves of sentences together.

1 Joey learned about Theo Goldman's money . . .
2 Joey left the house late at night . . .
3 When Goldman came into the back room, . . .
4 When Goldman hit Joey with the oil lamp, . . .
5 Joey saw the flames and the smoke . . .
6 Joey was a happy young man in Southampton . . .
7 . . . it broke and fell on the floor.

8 . . . but he did not go back to the shop.

9 . . . when Goldman told his friend about it in the pub.

10 . . . because he had a ticket for the *Titanic*.

11 . . . Joey pulled his arm up behind his back.

12 . . . and walked quickly to Goldman's shop.

Read *Hush Money* to the bottom of page 33. Can you guess what happens next? Choose answers to these questions.

1 What does the woman in the green coat want to do?

   a) She wants to take Rosa's photo.

   b) She wants to take Rosa to the police station.

   c) She wants to get money from the man.

   d) She wants to get money from Rosa.

2 What happens next?

   a) Rosa runs away.

   b) The man calls the police.

   c) The woman gets her money back.

   d) Rosa gives half of the man's money to the woman.

3 What does Rosa do after she leaves the car park?

   a) She has an accident in her car.

   b) She goes to the police.

   c) She stops asking people for hush money.

   d) She starts to work with the woman in the green coat.

After Reading

1 **Here are three characters – one from each story. Who are they, and what are they thinking about? Complete the passages with the words below (one word for each gap).**

afraid, anybody, called, come, easy, felt, find, for, hit, matter, money, night, pounds, pretty, real, sister, soon, Sunday, think, tried, wait, who

1 Marcia has a younger _____! She's a very _____ girl too.
I _____ not to look at her too much, but it wasn't _____.
And she _____ me good-looking! I _____ good when she
said that. But, really, Marcia is the one _____ me.

2 _____ is he, this Joe Smith? And is that his _____ name?
I don't think so – but it doesn't _____. I'm interested in
his _____, not his name. And where's he going to _____
a week's money on a _____? Well, I'm not going to
_____. He gives me the money _____, or he goes.

3 Not a good _____! I've got a bad head, and that
woman's got my fifty _____. But – where did she _____
from? I didn't see _____ in the car park. Perhaps my car
didn't _____ her. I was drunk and _____, so I didn't stop
and _____. She's a clever woman – but I can be clever
too . . .

2 **Here is a new illustration for one of the stories. Find the best place to put the picture, and answer these questions.**

The picture goes on page _____, in the story _____.

1 Who is this person?
2 What or who is she photographing?
3 Why is she doing this?

Now write a caption for the illustration.

Caption: _____

3 Use the clues below to complete this crossword with words from the story. Then find the hidden nine-letter word in the crossword, and answer the question about it.

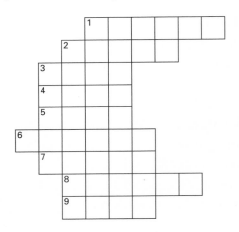

1 Karin liked to wear this in the roof garden.

2 You can drink wine or water from this.

3 To take something quickly.

4 Joey had a lot of this.

5 Rosa didn't have real accidents – she was a _____.

6 Joey broke the glass with this.

7 To look at somebody for a long time.

8 Rosa had some red _____ in a bottle in her pocket.

9 To fall after you put your foot on something wet.

The hidden word is _____.

Who uses this, in which story, and why?

4 **What does Karin say to Howard on the day when they are late? Put their conversation in the right order, and write in the speakers' names. Karin speaks first (number 3).**

1 _____ 'Well, no, I don't, but . . .'

2 _____ 'Of course not. It's a secret – our secret.'

3 _____ 'It's a lovely evening, Howard. Do you need to get home quickly?'

4 _____ 'So which way to this pub, then?'

5 _____ 'But Marcia wouldn't like it, Karin.'

6 _____ 'All right – but don't say anything to Marcia.'

7 _____ 'Marcia isn't here, Howard – but I am. Just a quiet drink – what's wrong with that?'

8 _____ 'How about a drink? I know a nice pub by the sea.'

5 **What happened after each story? Write the answer you like best using the notes (or write your own).**

· Police / find / bottle / take Marcia away // Howard / die / broken heart // Marcia / go / prison

· Marcia's father / die // Marcia / marry / Howard // Howard / always good / to her

· Joey / die / on *Titanic* // No more luck

· Joey / not die / *Titanic* // America / lots of luck / rich!

· Rosa / make friends / hospital // Better job / stop blackmail

· Rosa / blackmail / again // Real accident / kill her

ABOUT THE AUTHOR

John Escott worked in business before becoming a writer. Since then he has written many books for readers of all ages, but enjoys writing crime and mystery thrillers most of all. He was born in Somerset, in the west of England, but now lives in Bournemouth on the south coast. When he is not working, he likes looking for long-forgotten books in small back-street bookshops, watching old Hollywood films on video, and walking for miles along empty beaches.

He has written or retold more than twenty stories for Oxford Bookworms. His original stories include *Goodbye, Mr Hollywood* (at Stage 1), *Dead Man's Island* (at Stage 2), and *Agatha Christie, Woman of Mystery* (at Stage 2), which is the true story of the life of perhaps the most famous crime author in the world.

OXFORD BOOKWORMS LIBRARY

Classics • Crime & Mystery • Factfiles • Fantasy & Horror
Human Interest • Playscripts • Thriller & Adventure
True Stories • World Stories

The OXFORD BOOKWORMS LIBRARY provides enjoyable reading in English, with a wide range of classic and modern fiction, non-fiction, and plays. It includes original and adapted texts in seven carefully graded language stages, which take learners from beginner to advanced level. An overview is given on the next pages.

All Stage 1 titles are available as audio recordings, as well as over eighty other titles from Starter to Stage 6. All Starters and many titles at Stages 1 to 4 are specially recommended for younger learners. Every Bookworm is illustrated, and Starters and Factfiles have full-colour illustrations.

The OXFORD BOOKWORMS LIBRARY also offers extensive support. Each book contains an introduction to the story, notes about the author, a glossary, and activities. Additional resources include tests and worksheets, and answers for these and for the activities in the books. There is advice on running a class library, using audio recordings, and the many ways of using Oxford Bookworms in reading programmes. Resource materials are available on the website <www.oup.com/bookworms>.

The *Oxford Bookworms Collection* is a series for advanced learners. It consists of volumes of short stories by well-known authors, both classic and modern. Texts are not abridged or adapted in any way, but carefully selected to be accessible to the advanced student.

You can find details and a full list of titles in the *Oxford Bookworms Library Catalogue* and *Oxford English Language Teaching Catalogues*, and on the website <www.oup.com/bookworms>.

THE OXFORD BOOKWORMS LIBRARY
GRADING AND SAMPLE EXTRACTS

STARTER • 250 HEADWORDS

present simple – present continuous – imperative –
can/cannot, must – *going to* (future) – simple gerunds …

Her phone is ringing – but where is it?

Sally gets out of bed and looks in her bag. No phone. She looks under the bed. No phone. Then she looks behind the door. There is her phone. Sally picks up her phone and answers it. *Sally's Phone*

STAGE 1 • 400 HEADWORDS

… past simple – coordination with *and, but, or* –
subordination with *before, after, when, because, so* …

I knew him in Persia. He was a famous builder and I worked with him there. For a time I was his friend, but not for long. When he came to Paris, I came after him – I wanted to watch him. He was a very clever, very dangerous man. *The Phantom of the Opera*

STAGE 2 • 700 HEADWORDS

… present perfect – *will* (future) – *(don't) have to, must not, could* –
comparison of adjectives – simple *if* clauses – past continuous –
tag questions – *ask/tell* + infinitive …

While I was writing these words in my diary, I decided what to do. I must try to escape. I shall try to get down the wall outside. The window is high above the ground, but I have to try. I shall take some of the gold with me – if I escape, perhaps it will be helpful later. *Dracula*

STAGE 3 • 1000 HEADWORDS

... should, may – present perfect continuous – *used to* – past perfect –
causative – relative clauses – indirect statements ...

Of course, it was most important that no one should see
Colin, Mary, or Dickon entering the secret garden. So Colin
gave orders to the gardeners that they must all keep away
from that part of the garden in future. ***The Secret Garden***

STAGE 4 • 1400 HEADWORDS

*... past perfect continuous – passive (simple forms) –
would* conditional clauses – indirect questions –
relatives with *where/when* – gerunds after prepositions/phrases ...

I was glad. Now Hyde could not show his face to the world
again. If he did, every honest man in London would be proud
to report him to the police. ***Dr Jekyll and Mr Hyde***

STAGE 5 • 1800 HEADWORDS

*... future continuous – future perfect –
passive (modals, continuous forms) –
would have* conditional clauses – modals + perfect infinitive ...

If he had spoken Estella's name, I would have hit him. I was so
angry with him, and so depressed about my future, that I could
not eat the breakfast. Instead I went straight to the old house.
Great Expectations

STAGE 6 • 2500 HEADWORDS

... passive (infinitives, gerunds) – advanced modal meanings –
clauses of concession, condition

When I stepped up to the piano, I was confident. It was as if I
knew that the prodigy side of me really did exist. And when I
started to play, I was so caught up in how lovely I looked that
I didn't worry how I would sound. ***The Joy Luck Club***

Sherlock Holmes and the Sport of Kings

SIR ARTHUR CONAN DOYLE

Retold by Jennifer Bassett

Horseracing is the sport of kings, perhaps because racehorses are very expensive animals. But when they win races, they can make a lot of money too – money for the owners, for the trainers, and for the people who put bets on them to win.

Silver Blaze is a young horse, but already the winner of many races. One night he disappears from his stables, and someone kills his trainer. The police want the killer, and the owner wants his horse, but they can't find them. So what do they do?

They write to 221B Baker Street, London, of course – to ask for the help of the great detective, Sherlock Holmes.

The Withered Arm

THOMAS HARDY

Retold by Jennifer Bassett

A woman and a man . . . words of love whispered on a summer night. Later, there is a child, but no wedding-ring. And then the man leaves the first woman, finds a younger woman, marries her . . . It's an old story.

Yes, it's an old, old story. It happens all the time – today, tomorrow, a hundred years ago. People don't change. But this story, set among the green hills of southern England, has something different about it. Perhaps it is only a dream, or perhaps it is magic – a kind of strange dark magic that begins in the world of dreams and phantoms . . .

The Invisible Boy

Sally Gardner

Orion
Children's Books

To Dominic
with very happy memories of Splodge

ORION CHILDREN'S BOOKS

First published in Great Britain in 2002 by Dolphin Paperbacks
Reissued in 2013 by Orion Children's Books
This edition published in 2016 by Hodder and Stoughton

6

Text and illustrations copyright © Sally Gardner, 2002

The moral right of the author and illustrator has been asserted.

A CIP catalogue record for this book
is available from the British Library.

ISBN 978 1 4440 1161 6

Printed and bound in Great Britain
by Clays Ltd, St Ives plc

The paper and board used in this book are
made from wood from responsible sources.

MIX
Paper from
responsible sources
FSC® C104740

Orion Children's Books
An imprint of
Hachette Children's Group
Part of Hodder and Stoughton
Carmelite House
50 Victoria Embankment
London EC4Y 0DZ

An Hachette UK Company
www.hachette.co.uk

www.hachettechildrens.co.uk

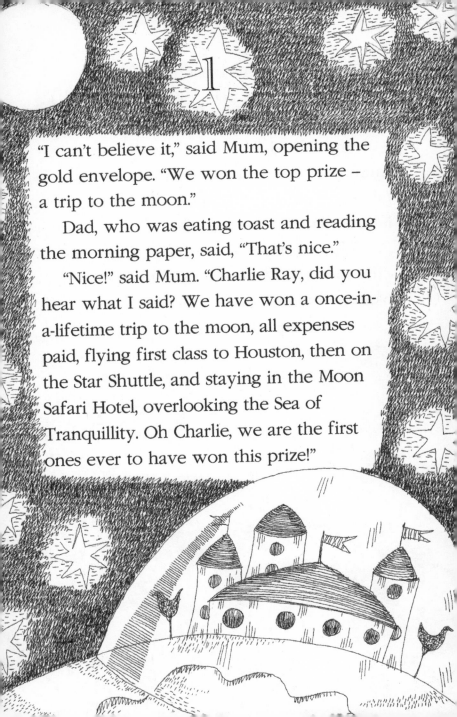

1

"I can't believe it," said Mum, opening the gold envelope. "We won the top prize – a trip to the moon."

Dad, who was eating toast and reading the morning paper, said, "That's nice."

"Nice!" said Mum. "Charlie Ray, did you hear what I said? We have won a once-in-a-lifetime trip to the moon, all expenses paid, flying first class to Houston, then on the Star Shuttle, and staying in the Moon Safari Hotel, overlooking the Sea of Tranquillity. Oh Charlie, we are the first ones ever to have won this prize!"

Dad dropped his toast and paper.

"Let me see," he said. "Oh Lily my love, I don't believe it. We are going to the moon!"

Sam walked into the room to find his mum and dad dancing round the kitchen table and singing "Fly me to the moon and let me play among the stars."

"What's going on?" said Sam, who was only half awake and unused to seeing his parents singing quite so loudly on a Saturday morning.

They told him the good news, both excited and talking at once, so that it took quite some time before they realised that children under twelve weren't allowed. It meant quite simply that Sam couldn't go.

"Well, that's that," said Dad after Mum had phoned to double-check with Dream Maker Tours.

"I will be fine," said Sam bravely. "Look, you must go. It's only for two weeks and I have lots of friends I can go and stay with, like Billy. I'm sure his mum won't mind."

2

The great day arrived. Mum and Dad were packed and ready to go when the phone rang. It was Billy Brand's mother, who was terribly sorry to say that Billy was not at all well. The doctor had just come round and said he had a very infectious virus. Sam couldn't possibly stay with him now. Mrs Brand hoped it hadn't ruined their trip.

"What are we going to do?" said Mum, putting down the last of the suitcases.

"I don't know," said Dad.

Just then the doorbell rang. Dad answered it. He was surprised to find their next-door neighbour, Mrs Hilda Hardbottom, standing there.

"I just popped round to see if you wanted the plants watering while you were away," she said, smiling.

"That's very kind of you,

8

Mrs Hardbottom, but I don't think we will be going after all," said Dad.

"What?" said Hilda, walking uninvited into the hall and closing the front door behind her. "Not going on a once-in-a-lifetime trip to the moon! Why not?"

Mum felt a bit silly. She should have got this better organised. "Sam's friend's mum has just rung to say he's not at all well, so Sam can't go to stay there," she said.

"Oh dear," said Mrs Hardbottom. "Still, that shouldn't stop you. Anyway you can't cancel, not now, with the eyes of the world on you, so to speak."

"We really have no choice, I can't leave Sam alone," said Mum.

"We must phone Dream Maker Tours right away and tell them we can't go," said Dad.

"There is no need to cancel. If it comes to that I can look after Sam," said Mrs Hardbottom firmly.

Mum and Dad were lost for words. They felt somewhat embarrassed. Mr and Mrs Hardbottom were their neighbours, and had been for years, but they really knew nothing about them, except they kept to themselves and seemed nice enough.

It was Sam who broke the awkward silence.

"That's the answer, Dad," he said, trying to sound cheerful.

Mum and Dad looked at one another then at Sam. Oh, how they loved their little boy! It broke their hearts seeing him being so grown-up and courageous.

"It's very kind of you, Mrs Hardbottom,
but…"

"Hilda," said Mrs Hardbottom, taking
control of the situation. At that moment
the doorbell rang. "No more buts," said
Hilda, opening the front door as if it were
her own house.

Plunket Road looked barely recognisable.
It was full of wellwishers and TV cameras.
Parked outside their front door was a
white shining limousine waiting to take
the Rays away.

A TV presenter with a games show
face walked into the hall where Mum and
Dad were standing. They both looked like
a couple of startled rabbits caught in the
headlights of an oncoming circus lorry.

"Mr and Mrs Ray, today is your day!
You are Dream Maker's out-of-this-world
winners!" said the presenter. "How does it
feel?"

Dad and Mum appeared to be frozen to the spot.

"Yes," said the presenter, "I too would be lost for words if I was lucky enough to be going to the moon."

Hilda spoke up. "They are a little sad to be leaving their son. But he is going to be fine, me and Ernie are going to look after him."

The camera panned on to Sam's face.

"You must be his kind and devoted granny," said the presenter, pleased at least that someone in the family had a voice.

"No," said Hilda, "I am the next door neighbour."

The presenter beamed his most plastic smile and his teeth shone like a neon sign. "Now isn't that what neighbours are for!" he said, putting an arm round Hilda and Sam.

Hilda was in heaven at being seen by forty million viewers world-wide. Mum and Dad smiled weakly. Nothing was agreed. This was all moving too fast.

"I brought round a disposable camera," Hilda continued. "I was hoping that my dear friends Charlie and Lily would take some nice pictures of the Sea of Tranquillity, for my Ernie. He wants to know what watersports they have up there on the moon."

"Well, isn't this cosy," said the presenter, handing the camera to Mum. He was now moving Mum and Dad out of the house into a sea of flashing camera lights, and somewhere in amongst all the chaos that was whirling around them, they found themselves parted from Sam. The white limousine whisked them away. The last thing they could see was Sam waving bravely.

There were two things at the top of Hilda
Hardbottom's wish list. They had been there
for forty years and hadn't until today shown
any sign of coming true. The first was to be
on TV, the second was to be rich.

"I don't know what's come over you,
sweetpea, you hate boys," said Ernie in a
stage whisper after Sam had gone to bed.
"You always said they smelt of old socks
that had been chewed by a dog."

"There is no need to whisper, Ernie
Hardbottom, unless I say whisper," she
snapped back at him.

Sam, who was trying to get to sleep
upstairs in the cold spare bedroom with
no curtains, heard Hilda's voice, and crept
to the top of the landing to see what was
going on. What he heard made going to
sleep even harder.

"Because, you numskull, how else was I ever going to star on TV?" said Hilda. "You have videotaped it, haven't you?"

"Yes, every minute of it, dearest," said Ernie.

"Good," said Hilda. Then she added as an afterthought, "Sam's parents must have taken out a lot of travel insurance, don't you think?"

"Well, if they haven't, Dream Maker Tours would have done, I imagine," said Ernie, pressing the play button on the video machine.

"Just think if anything were to go wrong with that Star Shuttle! Think of all that insurance money," said Hilda, rubbing her hands together with glee.

"That's not very nice," said Ernie.

"Who said anything about being nice," said Hilda, a wicked grin spreading across her face.

17

Sam went back to his cold lumpy bed. Tears welled up in his eyes. Oh, how he hoped that nothing would go wrong and that his mum and dad would soon be safely home!

The next day Sam went back to school and only had to be with Hilda and Ernie in the evening. All the evenings were long and dull. There was never enough to eat. After tea they would all sit together watching TV, and Hilda would hand out some of her homemade treacle toffee. The first night Sam had been so hungry that he had made the mistake of taking a piece. To his horror his mouth seemed to stick

together so he could hardly swallow, let alone speak. All he could do was sit there trying to finish the treacle toffee while listening to Ernie snoring and Hilda's stomach gurgling like an old dishwasher.

Bedtime couldn't come soon enough. Every night Sam would thank the stars that it was one day nearer to his mum and dad coming home.

But then, on the day his parents were due to return to earth, the unthinkable happened. Houston said they had lost all contact with the Star Shuttle. They were hoping it was just computer failure. The slow, mournful hours passed and the Star Shuttle still couldn't be found. Finally a spokesman for Dream Maker Tours announced on the six o'clock news that the Star Shuttle was missing.

5

The next morning Sam got ready to go to school. He would tell his teachers that he couldn't stay with the Hardbottoms any longer. He had lots of friends at school. He was sure someone would help him while this terrible mess was sorted out.

Hilda must have known what he was planning, for she was waiting for him by the front door, wearing her iron face. "Where do you think you're off to?"

"School," said Sam.

"No you're not. It's out of the question. Not at this sad time," said Hilda firmly.

"I can't stay here, I mean I was only supposed to be with you until my mum and dad got home," said Sam.

"Well, they're not home, are they, so it looks as if you're stuck with us," Hilda said smugly.

"But…" said Sam.

"The buts will have to make their own toast," said Hilda, pushing him back upstairs into his room.

The next few days passed in a haze. Hilda didn't allow him to go to school, or even out of the house alone, not with all the press and TV camped in their front garden. Sam Ray's parents were a hot story. Sam's picture appeared on every TV, newspaper, and Internet site in the world. Sam just remembered flashing lights and Hilda and Ernie being called the nation's favourite neighbours.

After a nailbiting week had passed, the officials at Houston said the Star Shuttle had been lost in space. All on board were presumed dead.

That was that. No more exciting pictures to be had. The TV and pressmen packed up and left.

Sam and his parents became yesterday's story. Old newspapers blowing around with the dead autumn leaves, and like them a thing of the past.

6

Hilda had liked the idea of being the nation's favourite neighbour and had made the most of it. She wore a kind and caring face that made the press and friends of the Rays say Sam was lucky to have Mr and Mrs Hardbottom to look after him. Especially as there were no living relatives.

But behind the thin disguise, Hilda was making plans. She had rented a cheap bungalow by the sea and made Ernie write a letter to Sam's school saying that they were taking Sam away on holiday, so that he would have a chance to get over his sad loss.

Hilda's plan was simple, and that was to get her hands on the Rays' insurance money. She wouldn't be able to do that if Sam said he didn't want to stay with them, and she couldn't keep him locked up forever. No, the best thing was to get right away. There were too many people offering to help. Mr Jenkins, who had mended Ernie's Ford Cortina, had said only the other week that he and his family would gladly look after Sam.

Ernie was a bit puzzled as to why Hilda was so keen to keep him.

"Why are you going to all the trouble and expense of booking a seaside holiday?" he asked. "We never go away."

"Because we can't stay here. People will begin to ask questions," said Hilda firmly.

"About what?" said Ernie scratching his head.

24

"About who is going to look after Sam," said Hilda beginning to lose her temper. "We don't want him saying he doesn't like it here."

"I'm sure he doesn't," said Ernie. "We can't look after him. We don't know anything about boys."

Hilda bristled like an old hairbrush. "I am only going to say this once more Ernie Hardbottom, and if it doesn't sink in to that sievelike brain of yours you can go and live in the potting shed with your CB radio for all I care."

Ernie looked at Hilda. She was not a pretty sight.

"The Rays," she said, talking to him as if he were five years old, "were insured for a lot of money by Dream Maker Tours, and now they are dead that money will go to Sam. Or to be more precise, to the guardians of Sam.

"If we play our cards right, that will be you and me."

"So we are going to adopt Sam," said Ernie, still not quite sure what Hilda was up to. "Don't you think, dearest, we are a little too old to be bringing up a boy?"

Hilda looked at Ernie as a cat might look at a mouse. "No," she said, "it means, you peabrain, that we are going to be rich."

"How do you make that out, sweetpea?" said Ernie, looking even more puzzled. "It's Sam's money, after all, and I don't think he would want to give it to us."

Hilda sighed. "I sometimes wonder how with a brain as small as yours you manage to keep going at all."

"That's not fair dearest," said Ernie in a small hurt voice.

"Oh, for pity's sake, life's not fair," said Hilda. "It is going to be our money and once we get our hands on it we are off to where the sun shines bright. Personally I am going to live the life I deserve. Sam can go whistle for his supper, and so can you if you don't buck up your ideas."

Ernie knew it was pointless to argue with Hilda. Once she got an idea in her head, it wasn't so much like watching a bull, rather a ten-ton lorry go through a china shop. Nothing was going to stop her.

7

That night Sam was unable to sleep. He looked out of his curtainless window at the back garden, with its neat rows of pumpkins, its potting shed, and its garden gnomes, lit up in the moonlight. He could even see the treehouse that Dad and he had made in his garden next door.

Sam flashed his torch up into the starry night sky. He had never felt more

abandoned. Space seemed to him so everlastingly vast. Where did it end? He felt tiny and invisible.

Sam lay down and tried to get to sleep. Suddenly there was a loud crash outside. He sat up in bed. All was quiet in the house. Sam was sure that if it had been an important crash, Hilda and Ernie would be up in a flash, but nothing stirred. Sam looked out of the window again. Everything looked the same, except that something was glowing in the pumpkin patch.

Sam tiptoed past Hilda and Ernie's bedroom. The door was ajar and Hilda's snores were loud enough to cover the noise of the creaking stairs. He went down to the back door and managed with great difficulty to get it open. He felt somewhat stupid standing in the garden, in the middle of the night, in his slippers and pyjamas. If he was caught now he would be in big trouble.

He walked slowly down the garden path. There, among the gnomes and the prize pumpkins, was what looked like a metal salad washer. A little like the one Hilda used to clean lettuce in, but bigger and a lot fancier. Whirring sounds were coming from it.

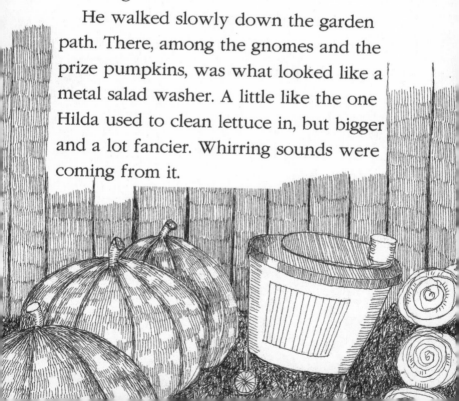

Then, to his horror, a gust of wind
blew the back door shut. He turned the
handle, but it wouldn't budge. He was
locked out.

Things were not looking good. This is
most definitely a dream, thought Sam. For
there, walking about bowing to the garden
gnomes, was an alien with green and
splodgy skin, saying, "Hello, I come in
peas. Take me to your chef."

When the gnomes didn't reply, the little alien, who was only a bit bigger than them, adjusted the two long pink tufts that stuck out of the top of his head and started again. "Hello, I come in peas..."

"Can I help?" asked Sam.

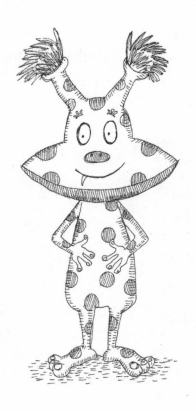

8

The little alien looked up, not in the least bit put off by someone so much bigger than himself. "My name is Splodge," he said. "I am from Planet Ten Rings. I come in peas."

"Good to see you. I am Sam Ray," said Sam.

"Are you the big chef?" asked Splodge.

"No," said Sam, "I am just a boy. I don't cook."

Splodge looked at him and then said, "One milacue, please." He ran back to where the metal salad washer lay and went inside.

"If this is a dream," said Sam to himself, "then why does it all seem so real?"

"Chief," said the alien, coming out, "take me to your chief."

"If you mean Mrs Hilda Hardbottom," said Sam, "I don't think she would be too pleased to see you."

Splodge leant on a flowerpot and muttered to himself. Then, pointing to the garden gnomes, he said, "Who are all those people? Are they prisoners of the Bottom?"

"No," said Sam, "they are plastic, I think, and they don't talk. They are just there to decorate the garden."

Splodge started to make a funny noise
and for one awful moment Sam thought
he was choking. He was not up on alien
first aid. Then, to his great relief, he realised
Splodge was laughing. Sam began to laugh
too. Splodge went over to where a gnome
was standing and gently pushed him over.
He started to laugh again.

"Ssh," said Sam, who didn't want Hilda
and Ernie waking up. "Why are you here?"
he asked.

Splodge looked at him as if he had
asked about the silliest question going.

"Sauce of the tomato 57," he said.

This was crazy, thought Sam. "You mean tomato ketchup? You have travelled all this way for that?"

"Yes," said Splodge. "I have travelled from Planet Ten Rings to bring home sauce of tomato 57 for my mum as a present for her," he thought hard for a moment, "hello nice to see you day."

"Like a birthday," said Sam.

"What's that?" asked Splodge.

"Oh, you know, the day you were born," Sam said.

"That's it," said Splodge. "A birthday mum present."

"I think you might be in the wrong place," said Sam. "You need a supermarket." He pointed in the direction of the shops. "It's about a kilometre down the road."

Splodge bowed. "Thankyourbits," he said, walking back towards the metal salad washer.

"By the way, what's that?" asked Sam.

"A spaceship," said Splodge,
disappearing inside. The door shut behind
him. Sam waited, not quite knowing what
to do. The spaceship started flashing with
bright colours. There was an alarming
whooshing sound as it started to rise. It
hovered two metres off the ground and
then crashed back down again. Another
loud bang followed, the door slid open,
and Splodge came out bottom first. The
two tufts on the top of his head were
now knotted together.

"Cubut flibnotted," he said.

Broken?" asked Sam.

The little alien nodded. "Whamdangled," he said sadly. "I need to make spaceship see-through."

"Do you mean invisible?" said Sam. "How can you do that?"

Suddenly a light went on in the house, and the curtains were pulled back to reveal Hilda and Ernie, lit up like figures in a toy theatre.

Splodge froze in fright. He had never seen such a scary sight before.

"That's the Bottoms hard?" he said.

"Yes," gulped Sam.

He looked down at Splodge, but to his surprise and alarm he had disappeared. Sam felt very scared, standing there all alone in the garden in the middle of the night in his dressing gown and slippers. How was he going to explain his way out of this one? His legs began to shake. Then to Sam's surprise he heard Splodge's voice.

"Hurry up," he said urgently, "it's invisible time."

"What?" said Sam. He couldn't see Splodge, but could feel something pulling on his pyjama bottoms.

"Hurry up," said Splodge again, "or you'll be whamdangled."

It was too late. The back door opened and there stood Ernie in his gumboots and Hilda in her rollers. She looked more frightening than any alien. She was flashing a torch round the garden. "I think it's that boy out there near the potting shed."

"Where?" said Ernie. "I can't see anything."

40

"That's because you are a short-sighted nincompoop," she hissed. "If that snivelling, smelly little toerag of a boy is out there he will be in big trouble."

"What are you doing?" said Splodge to Sam. "Now invisible time."

"I can't," said Sam desperately.

It was then that he felt Splodge press something onto his leg and the next thing he knew was that he was completely invisible, except for his slippers, which refused to disappear.

"I think you were seeing things," said Ernie, who just wanted to go back to his warm bed.

"I don't see things," said Hilda flatly. "Put your glasses on, and have a proper look.

Come on, I don't want to be standing out here all night."

"All right, all right," said Ernie, taking the torch from her. "Oh yes, I think I see something, sweetpea."

"What?" said Hilda, following Ernie.

Sam was frozen to the spot. His slippers seemed to shine out in the moonlight like a neon sign. Hilda and Ernie were moving straight towards him.

"I just..." started Sam.

Ernie looked round. "Did you say anything, dear?"

"Don't be daft, Ernie. Just keep walking," snapped Hilda.

It slowly began to dawn on Sam that he really was invisible and it wasn't his slippers that had caught Ernie's eye, it was the spaceship. Sam started to walk quickly back towards the open back door, his heart thumping so loud that he was sure that even if Hilda couldn't see him, she could hear him. He went into the house, Splodge still clinging on to his leg. Once he was safely inside, Sam shut and locked the back door.

10

Splodge stood in the kitchen tapping his foot. "See now you," he said impatiently to Sam, but all that could be seen of Sam were his dressing gown and slippers. Sam himself was completely invisible.

Sam was enjoying this and he was beginning to think that being invisible might just be the answer to all his problems. He would now be able to escape from the Hardbottoms and get help. That was until he caught sight of himself in the hall mirror. There was nothing to see. How would anyone know he was Sam Ray if he was invisible?

Suddenly there was

a loud noise from behind him. Sam turned round to see Splodge fiddling with a radio. Sam quickly turned it off.

"Flibnotted! Fandangled! Need radio," said Splodge urgently, pulling one of his tufts. "Must understand you better."

Hilda and Ernie were now banging with all their might on the back door.

Sam picked up Splodge and went upstairs to his room and got out his Walkman. Splodge put one earpiece in each tuft, then closed his eyes, folded his arms over his fat little tummy and listened. After a minute or two he started singing at the top of his voice.

"Hip hop it never will stop,

This planet can rock the stars.
Hip hop this never will stop.
We are the men from Mars."

"Not so loud," said Sam desperately to
Splodge, who said, "Like the music, dude, it
rocks. So tell me, why don't you know
how to do visible-invisible? Do you have
learning difficulties?"

"No," said Sam, "we humans don't do
that." He was beginning to feel a little
worried. "What did you put on me in the
garden?" he said.

"My one and only patch," said Splodge.
"I was going to use it on my spaceship,
but when I saw the Bottom hard, and
you not doing anything to escape, I did
what any other Splodgerdite would have
done, helped you out. Because, my H
bean, you had gone and forgotten how to
go invisible."

"No," said Sam, "I keep telling you we

humans don't do invisible."

"How do you live?" said Splodge with great feeling, as if this was a design fault that should have been mastered years ago. "It must be something awful to be seen all the time."

"It is," said Sam.

"To a Splodgerdite," said Splodge, yawning, "being invisible is like moving leglot. It's just what we do."

"Sorry," said Sam, "you lost me."

Splodge lifted one of his little legs and pointed. "Leglot."

"You mean leg," said Sam.

"Yes," said Splodge. "It's

easy peasy, once you get the handangle of it. Like learning languages." He was now making himself a bed in Hilda's old sock basket. "Next day when the sun comes up to see you," he said sleepily, "I get my spaceship back."

"Will I be visible again tomorrow?" said Sam, but Splodge was fast asleep.

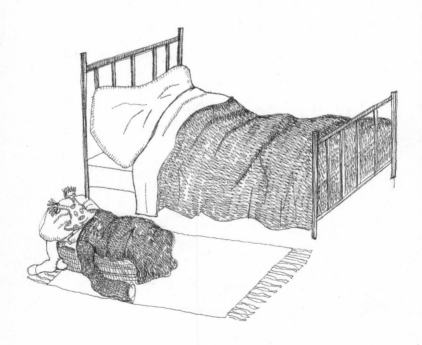

11

Sam woke to find he was quite normal again. He brushed his teeth, washed and got dressed, thinking all the time how wicked it would be if he was really invisible, and went downstairs for breakfast.

He was surprised to see that there were suitcases in the hall, and that Hilda was busy packing tins of food into boxes, which Ernie was taking out to the car. Perhaps, thought Sam, they were leaving and he would finally be able to get away. It was then that he noticed that the back door had a panel missing from it. He was about to ask how that had happened, but the look on Hilda's face told him it wouldn't be a good idea.

"Now listen to me," she said, loading Ernie up with another box. "We are taking you to the seaside for a few days for a holiday."

"I don't want to go, I can't go," said Sam, feeling panicky. "I mean I don't want to leave my house, in case my mum and dad get back and can't find me."

"He's got a point, lambkin," said Ernie resting the box on the edge of the kitchen table. "Anyway, who's going to water my prize pumpkins?"

"You keep out of this, Ernie Hardbottom," said Hilda firmly. "Now you listen to me, young man. Your mum and dad are not coming back ever. The sooner you get that into your head the better."

Sam could feel tears burning at the back of his eyes.

"You should be grateful," said Hilda, picking up the metal salad washer and putting it on top of the box Ernie was carrying, "that we are going to all this trouble just for you."

"There's no need," said Sam desperately. "Why don't you go, and I can stay with a friend?"

Hilda's face twisted into that of a witch.

Sam wasn't going to cry in front of her. He looked again at the metal salad washer. He was sure he had seen it before.

"Where did you get this?" he asked, picking it up.

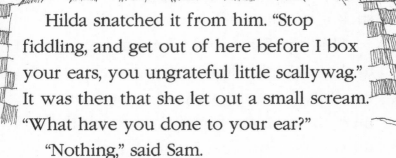

Hilda snatched it from him. "Stop fiddling, and get out of here before I box your ears, you ungrateful little scallywag." It was then that she let out a small scream. "What have you done to your ear?"

"Nothing," said Sam.

"Shouldn't boys have two ears, dearest?" said Ernie.

"Of course they should, peabrain." She pulled Sam over to the mirror. Sure enough one of his ears was invisible, although he could still feel it.

"Perhaps it fell off," said Ernie. "I think we'd better start looking for it, and then take him to the hospital to see if they can stick it back again."

"Shut up, Ernie, and take that box out to the car," said Hilda, looking at Sam carefully. "Are you playing games with me?" she said, reaching out to touch the missing ear. Sam moved away fast.

"I think Ernie's right, we should stay here," said Sam.

"Oh you do, do you?" said Hilda, folding her arms over her ample chest. "Well, I'm not fooled by your little joke. Now get upstairs and pack, and by the way, if you see your missing ear bring it with you."

12

Sam's only comforting
thought was that perhaps it
wasn't a dream, in which case he should
find an alien called Splodge sleeping in the
sewing basket. To his delight and great
relief, there he was, curled up into a ball.

"Good moon to you," said Splodge,
stretching out his little arms.

"We're off, come down here now,"
shouted Hilda.

"Is that the call of the Bottom hard?"
asked Splodge sleepily.

"Look," said Sam, "I don't want to go,
but they are taking me to the seaside and
I can't leave you here all alone."

"I can't leave my spaceship," said
Splodge, "so I suppose this is toodleoo."

"Then I've got bad news," said Sam. "It's
packed in the car that's taking me away.

Hilda thinks it's a salad washer."

Splodge sat up and looked at Sam.
"That's a first rate spaceship," he said.

Hilda's voice had got louder and nastier.
"If I have to come up and get you, there
will be big trouble. Do you hear me, boy?"

Without another word Splodge got up,
made his way over to the rucksack and
climbed in. "The one good thing is that
you're visible again," he said, making
himself comfortable.

"Apart from one ear," said Sam, picking
up his rucksack.

"What's an ear between aliens?" said
Splodge.

The Ford Cortina was packed to
bursting. Ernie was so small that he had to
sit on three cushions before he could see
over the wheel. Sam wondered why Hilda
didn't drive, as she was the one that gave
all the instructions.

"You are going too fast, keep over to
the left, no you shouldn't be in that gear."

All Ernie would say was a feeble, "Yes
dear, no dear."

It took the best part of a day to get to
Skipton-on-Sea and when they finally
arrived, smoke was coming out of the

bonnet of the car. It came to a grinding halt
outside a dismal-looking bungalow that
smelt of damp and was colder inside than it
was out. Why anyone would come here for
a holiday was beyond Sam. His heart sank.

"This will do very nicely," said Hilda.

"Well," said Ernie, "the sea air must
agree with our Sam because look,
sweetpea, his ear is back again."

"Of course it is," snapped Hilda. "It was
only that smelly little toerag's idea of a
joke and I don't laugh that easily."

"No," said Ernie, "no, you don't."

13

It was hard to imagine a more miserable and isolated place. Even when tea was made and the lights turned on it had the feeling of being at the end of the world, and there was no way back.

Sam's room was smaller than the last one, and worst of all, the walls seemed to be made of paper. He could hear every word of what Hilda and Ernie had to say and none of it was good. Finally he could hear Hilda snoring, and he knew he was safe to look in his rucksack. He wanted to make sure he hadn't gone completely mad that morning imagining an alien, and a spaceship that looked like a salad washer. It was the only thing that had given him hope, as they drove farther and farther away from his home, from all that he knew and loved.

Sam emptied his rucksack carefully. There was no Splodge. He must have imagined it. He looked again. There were only the few things he had packed this morning. He turned it inside out. Tears started to roll down his face. He should have run away before they kidnapped him. Now Sam was lost just like his mum and dad.

He was lying in bed wondering, if he ran away, would he be able to find his way back, when the bedroom door opened all by itself.

Sam sat up in bed and flashed his torch. There, slowly making its way across the floor, without anyone helping it, was a bottle of tomato ketchup.

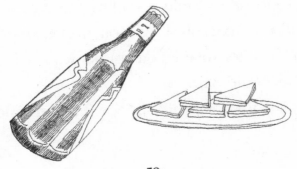

It came to a stop, and then Sam heard the padding of little feet and saw a plate of finger-size sandwiches wobbling in the air. They tottered one way, then another. Sam shone his torch on to the plate. A small voice said, "Stop it, I can't see."

"Is that you, Splodge?" said Sam hopefully.

"Who else," said Splodge, becoming visible again, with the plate of sandwiches in his hands. Sam had never been so pleased to see an alien before.

"These," said Splodge proudly, "are for you. Sandwiches of tomato ketchup and pea butter with nut."

Sam was so hungry that he ate them all down. They tasted great.

"Good news," said Splodge, "I have found my spaceship. Bad bit, wet inside."

"That's because Hilda thinks it's a salad washer," said Sam.

"It's a Viszler Junior Space Carrier," said

Splodge, sounding offended, "and that monster alien thinks it's a salad washer, whatever that may be."

"It's something you put lettuce in and then you whizz it around and hey presto you have clean lettuce," said Sam, finishing the last of the sandwiches.

"Or hay pisboo you have a broken spaceship," said Splodge.

"I'm sorry," said Sam.

Splodge didn't look up. He was busy, comforting himself by sucking the tomato ketchup out of the bottle.

14

For the first time since coming to stay with the Hardbottoms, Sam didn't feel alone. He sat on the bed with Splodge, looking out of the window. The moon looked like a big balloon that had come to rest on the garden wall.

Sam told Splodge about his parents' disastrous trip and how everyone thought they were dead and lost in space.

Splodge tutted. "I shouldn't think so, they most probably got stuck inside a grotter. Has anybody gone and looked?"

"What's that?" asked Sam.

"Surely you know what a grotter is," said Splodge.

"No I don't," said Sam. "I haven't a clue, what is it?"

Splodge looked worried. "Don't you learn anything at school then?"

"Maths, English, and history, mainly boring things like that," said Sam.

"Not about the planets, and the stars, and space dragons?" said Splodge. "Or how to look after a grotter, and what to do if an orgback turns up?"

"No," said Sam, who thought he would much rather learn about space than William the Conqueror.

"Grotters," continued Splodge, "are black as space and hard to see. They have huge tum tums and float about with their mouths wide open feeding on metricels of light, gaggerling up whatever gets in their way."

Sam looked at Splodge, still not understanding what he was talking about.

"Planet Ten Rings," explained Splodge," is milacue. So we look after the grotters and they look after us. Keep the orgbacks away, for a start."

"What are they?" said Sam.

"Humungous space monsters that can gaggerly up whole stars," said Splodge.

"Why don't you think an orgback swallowed the Star Shuttle then?" said Sam.

"Not possible, they live deep in space and we hardly ever see them. They wouldn't be bothered with a smidger of a thing like a spaceship. It wouldn't be worth munching."

"Would a Star Shuttle be all right inside a grotter or would that be the end of it?" asked Sam anxiously.

"More likely to make a grotter tum
feel all wobbly and wonky," said
Splodge. "I need to get a message home
to my mum and dad. Then I would be
able to tell them about the Star Shuttle."

But the problem was, how were they
going to do that, now Splodge's
spaceship was broken.

15

The morning did not bring with it a cheerful picture of holiday bliss. Thin drizzle fell and Sam could not see the sea because of a cement wall that blocked out the view. All the neighbouring bungalows were boarded up.

Hilda was busy trying to sort out the kitchen. "Did you get up in the night and take some food?" she said in a menacing voice.

"No," said Sam.

"Well, there are breadcrumbs where breadcrumbs shouldn't be," said Hilda.

"Perhaps there's mice," said Sam.

Hilda picked up the broom and shook it at Sam. "I don't want any more of your cheek, you little toerag. Go out and play."

"It's raining," said Sam.

"Out!" shouted Hilda.

Sam went out into the back yard. You couldn't call it a garden. It had high walls and crazy paving, and looked more like a prison yard. In it were two broken garden chairs, a washing line with a mouldy dishcloth hanging from it, and a pot with some tired plastic flowers sticking out of it.

Ernie was in the tiny shed at the back, fiddling about with wires.

"What are you doing?" asked Sam.

Ernie nearly jumped out of his skin. "Nothing, dear, nothing," he said. "Oh, it's you. What do you want?"

"It's raining," said Sam.

"Oh all right, you can stay here, but don't fiddle," said Ernie.

"What's that?" asked Sam, pointing to a funny-looking machine.

"It's a citizen's band radio," said Ernie, beaming with pride as he showed Sam how it worked. "It's not like your everyday radio. Before I retired I used to

drive long distance lorries, and this is how
we talked to each other. We all had
different names." Ernie blushed and said,
"I was called Tiger Raw. Sometimes if I
was lucky, I would be able to pick up
signals on it from as far away as Russia
and beyond. Isn't she beautiful!"

"Could it send messages into space?"
asked Sam eagerly.

"I don't rightly know," said Ernie,
scratching the top of his head. "That's a

mighty long way away, isn't it. I mean, it's farther than Russia."

"Only a little bit," said Sam.

"Anyway, I've just bought a bigger receiver," said Ernie, "but I'm having trouble wiring it up. The instructions seem to be written in double Dutch," he said sadly, looking at the manual.

"Ernie, where are you?" shouted Hilda.

"Out here, sweetpea," called Ernie.

"What are you doing?"

"Nothing, dearest, just fiddling," said Ernie.

"Stop it right now," shouted Hilda, "and come in here and help me make pea soup. And you too," Hilda shouted at Sam.

An awful smell of overcooked vegetables greeted them as they walked into the kitchen.

"I want you to stir this," said Hilda, showing Sam a pot of smelly, slimy green liquid. "Don't let it stick to the bottom. That soup is going to have to last us a week."

Sam sighed, and did as he was told. It was then that he realised both his hands were going invisible.

"Hilda," said Ernie, staring at Sam, "do you think boys fade away when they are unhappy?"

"What gibberish are you talking now, Ernie?" said Hilda.

"Sam's hands. They've gone and vanished," said Ernie.

Hilda turned on Sam. "You are doing this on purpose, aren't you, you ungrateful boy, and after all the trouble that we've gone to!"

"I just want to go home," said Sam bravely. "I shouldn't be here."

"He's got a point, dearest," said Ernie.

Hilda looked more frightening than an old flesh-eating dinosaur, all red and furious. "You keep out of this, you peabrain," she snapped, towering over Sam. "You'd better stay in your room until you learn not to play any more of these jokes, or you'll be sorry you were ever born."

16

Splodge was on the bed, listening to Sam's Walkman, and finishing off the last of the tomato ketchup.

"The good news," said Sam, sitting down next to him, "is that Ernie has a radio and a powerful receiver which he can't work. It just might get a message back to your planet. The bad news is, I'm grounded until my hands become visible again."

"It's going to be a long time then," said Splodge.

Sam was slowly fading away. By teatime he was completely invisible. All that could be seen of him were his clothes.

"I don't think I should have stuck that patch on you, " said Splodge anxiously. "It was meant for spacecraft, not for H beans."

"Stop worrying," said Sam. "Look, last time I came back, so why wouldn't it happen again?"

Splodge tried explaining about invisibility, but it was no use, Sam was far too excited, working out the best combination for frightening the pants off Hilda Hardbottom.

"Hi," he said calmly, walking into the kitchen for tea. "I am so hungry I am almost fading away."

Ernie and Hilda nearly jumped out of their skins when they saw a cap and a pair of trousers coming towards them.

"I don't think this is right, dearest," said Ernie, dropping the newspaper. "Shouldn't we be able to see him?"

"Of course we should," said Hilda shakily.

"I think it might be best to take him home, and get a doctor to have a look at him," said Ernie.

"What do you think would happen, you ninny, if we went home with an invisible boy?" said Hilda,

"I don't know, sweetpea," said Ernie.

Hilda sat down at the kitchen table. She was really worried. This wasn't in her grand plan. In fact she could be accused of causing Sam's disappearance. Then they would be in deep trouble. Hilda couldn't allow her plan to go wrong, not now when she was so close to getting what she wanted. Maureen Cook from Dream Maker Tours had said it was only a matter of her seeing Sam, then the money would be as good as theirs.

"Remember the ear, sweetpea, it came back," said Ernie, trying to sound encouraging.

Hilda filled their bowls with green slimy pea soup.

"Eat up," she said, putting on her TV face, "we don't want you fading away altogether now, do we."

Sam took off his cap and put it on the table. Hilda jumped back. There was now nothing to show that Sam was sitting in his seat, except a spoon playing with the slimy soup.

"I don't much like pea soup," said Sam, who was enjoying seeing Hilda squirm.

"What do you like?" said Hilda nervously. "You can have anything you want as long as it helps make you visible again."

So Sam gave her a long list, starting with twelve small bottles of tomato ketchup.

17

That night Hilda couldn't sleep. She was walking up and down in the lounge when a picture came off the wall right in front of her, and a china dog started to move across the mantelpiece. Sam was having fun.

"Is that you, Sam?" she said in a shaky voice. Sam didn't answer. Splodge, who was also invisible, was tickling her leg. She let out a scream and Ernie came in, yawning. What he saw made his legs wobbly with fright. A chair was floating round the room.

"That's not right," said Ernie, "I mean, chairs don't do that, do they?"

The chair dropped to the ground with a thud.

"Of course they don't, you ninny," Hilda said trembling.

"You know, sweetpea," said Ernie, "I think this place might be haunted. I just felt a rush of cold air." The lounge door closed with a bang.

Hilda recovered herself. "Of course it's not haunted," she snapped, picking up a cushion and hitting out at thin air. "Take that, you little toerag," she shouted. But Sam and Splodge had left, and were safely out of the way in the shed.

"I like being invisible," said Sam. "The only drawback is that it's chilly without your clothes on."

"Pish bosh, you're supposed to come and go, not stay like that all the time," said Splodge. "The sooner we get a message home the better."

The CB radio was not working that well, mainly because it had been wired to the receiver the wrong way. It took

Splodge some time to get it sorted out.

"Come on," said Sam, "I'm getting chilly out here."

"Well go back to the monster grotto then," said Splodge, "and make us something to fill up gurgling tummy."

The radio was now making strange noises and Splodge kept moving the knobs and listening. Then he started speaking in a language that Sam couldn't understand.

"Χαλλινγ Πλανεντ τεν ρινγσ"

Sam walked back towards the bungalow. The lounge looked as if a giant hippo had had hysterics. Hilda had finally gone to bed exhausted, and was snoring like a battleship attacking her enemy.

The great thing about being invisible, thought Sam, opening the fridge and looking inside, is that I don't feel frightened any more. I have some power and that is a truly wicked feeling. He poured out all the milk there was into two glasses, made a pile of peanut butter sandwiches and found the last bottle of tomato ketchup.

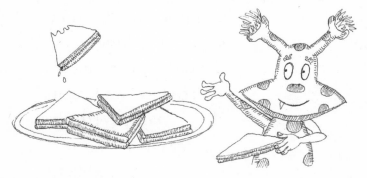

"I've got message home," said Splodge, becoming visible again. "They've heard of a sick grotter, in fact it's caused quite a hollerburluke. Something is definitely stuck inside it. They're on their way out to it. Also my mum says not to worry and sends you her toodle hyes."

"Oh that's wonderful," said Sam.
"So what will happen now?"

"Mum and Dad want to say hi and talk
to me again tomorrow. Also I've got to tell
them about the invisible problem,"
mumbled Splodge. "I'm sure my dad
and mum can think of something."

18

The bungalow was unusually quiet the next morning. Hilda had taken the car into the village to do some shopping, and Ernie was in the shed, playing with his radio. To his delight it was working better than it had ever done before, picking up some very strange sounds, "Χαλλινγ σπλογε σπαχε σηυττλε ρχοϖερεδ αλλ ον βοαρδ αρε σαφε."

Sam and Splodge spent the best part of the morning in the lounge. Sam was still invisible, but today he was dressed. It was too chilly to walk about without your clothes on. They sat together on the beaten up

sofa, eating cereal out of the packet, watching whatever they wanted on TV.

Ernie, who had been left with strict instructions not to let Sam out of his sight, kept coming in from the shed, and saying, "You all right then?" On one of these visits he was sure he saw a green spotty little fellow sitting next to Sam, but then again he might just be seeing things, he hadn't got his glasses on, and the next time he looked it had gone.

About two o'clock the phone rang. Ernie picked it up. It was Maureen Cook from Dream Maker Tours. She couldn't have sounded more helpful, and said she would be coming down to see Sam tomorrow, to talk about his future.

"That will be nice," said Ernie, putting down the phone and telling Sam what she had just said.

"Do you think she will recognise me?" asked Sam.

"Oh dear," said Ernie. "Oh dear, I forgot you were invisible."

Hilda was not in a good mood when she arrived home at teatime, weighed down by shopping bags. Her mood was not improved one little bit when Ernie told her about Maureen Cook. She started rumbling like an old boiler ready to burst.

"You are worse than hopeless, you peabrain," she said to Ernie, who was looking very sheepish. "What are we going to show her, an invisible boy?"

"Perhaps," said Sam, "if you were kind to me, I might become visible again."

"It's worth a try," said Ernie in a small shaky voice.

Hilda said nothing, but banged and thumped round the kitchen unpacking the shopping.

"Oh that looks nice, sweetpea," said Ernie, seeing all the things Sam had asked for, including the twelve bottles of tomato ketchup.

"Well, none of it's for you," she snapped at Ernie. "It isn't you that's invisible, more's the pity." She handed Sam a bag. "Put these on," she ordered.

In it were a woolly balaclava, a pair of multi-coloured gloves, a cheap pair of dark glasses, and as the finishing touch, a pair of plastic joke lips.

"What are these for?" said Sam, laughing.

"This isn't funny," said Hilda. "Just do as I say."

When he saw himself in the hall mirror he couldn't stop laughing. Oh, now he really did look scary, as if he were about to rob a bank. Roll on tomorrow, he thought. How was Hilda going to get out of this mess?

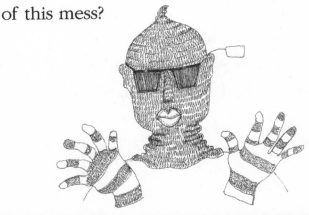

19

The reason, Splodge said, that Splodgerdites adored tomato ketchup was simple. It was the sauce of their good looks, it kept them young, healthy, and wise. Also, growing tomatoes was unheard of on Planet Ten Rings. It was only on earth that the tomato could be transformed into the right stuff for aliens.

"Have you been here lots of times, then?" asked Sam.

Splodge looked down at his toes. "No," he said, "I have only been here once before with my dad, and it was a short sort of visit."

It turned out that Splodge was only about as old as Sam, and that this was the first time he had travelled on his own to earth.

"I thought I would get my mum a present," said Splodge sadly, "but it all went a bit starshaped. I am only a junior space flyer, I start my AST course next year."

"What's that?" asked Sam.

"Advanced Space Travel," said Splodge. "That's when we learn everything to do with space and all the other things like grotters and orgbacks."

Sam didn't like to ask, he had a nasty feeling he already knew the answer.

"Have you ever used one of those invisible patches before?" he said.

"No," said Splodge.

"Do you know what happens when one of those patches is put on a boy like me?" asked Sam.

"No," said Splodge, looking a little shamefaced. "They are only to be used when everything is whamdangled."

Sam was beginning to feel panicky. It was one thing to be invisible for a few days, but not forever. What if his parents came back? How would they know it was Sam if they couldn't see him?

"Will I ever be visible again?" asked Sam anxiously.

"Need to speak to Dad," said Splodge. "I'm sure someone on Ten Rings will know what to do."

But it was proving to be quite difficult to get a message home. Ernie had been fiddling again with the radio and it took Splodge ages to pick up a signal, and then he could hardly hear what they were saying, except for the odd word like σουνδ σηυττλε σαφε.

"We'll have to try again tomorrow," said
Sam, seeing the look on Splodge's face. He
was tired and his bright green skin was
losing its shine.

"Pish bosh, I want to go home," he said
sadly. "I miss my mum."

"I know," said Sam. He took Splodge
back to the house, gave him a bottle of
tomato ketchup and tucked him up in bed.

"So do I," said Sam quietly. "I miss Mum
and Dad very much indeed."

20

The next day the Hardbottoms were up early, cleaning and tidying the bungalow.

Hilda put on her smiling face that she kept at the bottom of an old make-up bag and only used for special occasions. Ernie put on his one and only suit. The tea had been set out on a tray in the lounge, and the curtains were drawn. Hilda had put

Sam in the armchair with a rug over his knees. When Ernie saw him sitting there in the balaclava and dark glasses and false lips, he jumped with fright.

"Hilda," he said, "there's a strange man sitting in the armchair.

He wasn't there a moment ago. Did you let him in? He looks very scarey!"

"That, you peabrain, is Sam," said Hilda.

When Maureen Cook arrived she was rather taken aback by the Hardbottoms' idea of a holiday. The bungalow was seedy, and smelt damp.

"You could have taken yourselves somewhere nice and hot," she said. "We would happily have paid."

"Didn't want to look too greedy," said Hilda, smiling. "Not until all this is settled, so to speak."

"Please remember," said Maureen, "Dream Maker Tours are here to make your dreams a reality."

"I hope so," said Hilda, taking Maureen through to the lounge, and placing her in the chair furthest away from Sam. Hilda handed her a cup of tea and a piece of cake, talking all the time, like a car alarm that wouldn't stop, about how much they cared for Sam and how he enjoyed sitting in the dark wearing a balaclava.

"It makes him feel protected from the outside world. Grief," said Hilda, "can do strange things to one."

"Please Mrs Hardbottom," said Maureen, "will you let me speak. Are you feeling all right, Sam?" she asked.

"As I said," interrupted Hilda, "Sam is a bit shy."

Sam nodded and mumbled, "I'm OK."

"Do you like it here?" Maureen started.

Hilda interrupted again. "These questions aren't too strenuous, are they?" she said, sounding concerned. "It's just that we care so much for the boy, and want to protect him. After all, I'm not called the Nation's Favourite Neighbour for nothing."

"Quite so," said Maureen, bringing a picture of Sam out of her briefcase, and going over to the window to draw back the curtains. "I would like to see your face,

Sam, if you don't mind."

"I do mind," said Hilda, rushing past her and standing in front of the window. "He has been through an awful lot, why does he have to answer these questions? Isn't it enough that he's here?"

"I am just doing my job, Mrs Hardbottom," said Maureen wearily. This wasn't going to plan. She had hoped to have all this sorted out in no time at all.

"Treacle toffee," said Hilda, holding out a sweet tin. "I made it myself."

Maureen smiled weakly. "Well, one piece if you insist, then I must ask Sam these questions."

Sam watched the look of horror spread over Maureen Cook's face as her jaws slowly stuck together and she was unable to say another word.

Hilda took her back to the chair farthest away from Sam.

"Shall we talk about the money?" said Hilda, smiling charmingly.

At that moment Ernie came into the room. "Wonderful news, sweetpea," he said. "The Star shuttle has made contact with Earth. I just heard it on my CB radio. It looks like Mr and Mrs Ray will be coming home after all."

"Hooray!" shouted Sam, sending the false pair of lips shooting across the room.

Maureen looked startled and Sam put his gloved hand across his mouth and said, "It's the best bit of news ever."

21

Maureen Cook had written out a cheque to cover their holiday expenses.

"Is that all?" said Hilda, seeing how little she had been given.

But Maureen was now running towards her car, still unable to speak, a hanky held over her mouth.

"Wait a minute, come back," shouted Hilda.

It was too late. Maureen sped off down the road at top speed.

"It's all your fault," Hilda screamed at Ernie. "If you hadn't come charging in like that, we would have been given loads of money."

Hilda marched like an invading army into the shed. She got hold of the CB radio, and lifted it high above her head.

"Don't do that!" shouted Ernie and Sam together. It was too late. Hilda threw it to the ground.

"I think," said Ernie sadly, "you've gone and broken it."

"I hope so," said Hilda. "If you had half a brain, you would have seen what I was trying to do instead of mucking up all my plans."

Hilda went back into the kitchen followed by Sam. All that could be seen of him now was a pair of dark glasses.

"You wretched boy, none of this would have happened if you hadn't gone invisible," yelled Hilda. "Well, you can stop playing games. I haven't come this far for you to ruin everything. You are going to become visible again and tell your mum and dad you had a lovely time with us.

Do you hear me?"

Sam, who had long lost his fear of
Hilda, said calmly, "I won't. I will tell them
the truth, that you are a mean, nasty two-
faced witch."

Hilda grabbed a broom. "What did you
call me?" she shouted, bringing it down
with a nasty crack on the sunglasses,
which fell broken to the floor.

At that moment Splodge walked
into the room, quite visible.

"I agree," he said.

Hilda dropped her
broom and scrambled up
on the table as fast as her
tubby legs would let her.
Splodge went over to
where the broken glasses
lay, and picked them up.

"You," said Splodge, "should be boggled."

Hilda started screaming at the top of her voice.

Ernie came in holding his smashed radio.

"Look!" yelled Hilda, pointing at Splodge. "It's a monster, a rat, an alien. Don't stand there, do something!"

If Ernie wasn't mistaken, this was the same little fellow that he had seen sitting with Sam the other day on the sofa.

"Well, what are you waiting for? I think that creature has murdered Sam!" said Hilda "Look at the smashed glasses."

Ernie said nothing. He had seen many frightening things in his life, though sadly none of them as frightening as his wife when she was in one of her moods.

"I can't see what all the fuss is about," said Sam, invisible from the other side of the room. "That's my friend Splodge, from Planet Ten Rings, and he's not best pleased that you have ruined his spaceship by filling it with water."

Hilda went white with fright. "Do something, Ernie," she pleaded.

For the first time since he had married Hilda, way back in the dark ages, Ernie felt brave. If a boy and a little alien could stand up to her, so could he.

"No, I won't," he said firmly. "You have gone too far this time, Hilda. I should have had the courage to stop you, but I didn't – more's the pity."

Splodge stepped forward. "You are a cruel and mean hard bottom, and you give earth H beans a bad name," he said, holding his little hands out before him. Bright green rays came out of his fingertips. Hilda's face went a horrid pink and then became covered in tiny green spots.

"Nice one," said Sam.

Hilda quickly climbed down off the table, ran into the hall, grabbed her coat and hat, stuffed the cheque into her handbag and ran out of the front door and down the street as fast as her stumpy legs would carry her.

22

On the TV that night, every programme was about the Star Shuttle's miraculous return to earth. Experts were talking about black holes and all sort of other theories to explain how a spaceship could go missing for so long. No one mentioned grotters or a small planet called Ten Rings.

Splodge had been spending the evening trying to wire the radio up to his spaceship in the hope of getting a message home, but it wasn't working. Ernie was out in the back yard with the receiver.

"Try it now," said Ernie.

There were a few beeping noises and then nothing.

"Pish bosh, it's hopeless," said Splodge sadly. "We are truly boggled."

"Often when things don't work," said Sam "my dad gives them a little tap. He says it helps them wake up."

"Go on then," said Splodge.

Sam tapped the top of the spaceship. Nothing happened.

"Well," said Splodge, "it doesn't work."

But that was as far as he got. The spaceship suddenly lit up. Sparks of rainbow colour came shooting out of it, lighting up the drab back yard.

"OW!" said Sam.

Then they all heard

Τηισ ισ πλανεντ τεν Ρινγσ Χαλλινγ Σπλοδγε

"That's my dad!" shouted Splodge.
"That's my dad!"

It was a much larger spacecraft that
landed in the back yard that night, and
Splodge's parents were thrilled to see their
son.

"This is Sam," said Splodge, looking
down at his toes. Sam held out the arm of
his old jumper.

"Oh dear," said Splodge's dad. "What
have you done, junior?"

"He was trying to protect me," said Sam.

"He didn't realise I couldn't go invisible."

"Sorry, Dad," said Splodge.

His dad smiled a kind smile. "Well, we'd better put it right."

He held out his hands and a blue light flashed around Sam. The next thing, there he was, visible again.

"Thank you," said Sam. "Oh, it's great to be seen again."

Ernie offered to make them tea, but Splodge's parents wanted to get home as soon as possible.

"Wait a minute, I can't go without Mum's present," said Splodge.

He rushed back into the bungalow and brought out twelve bottles of tomato ketchup.

"These are for you, Mum," said Splodge.

She gave him a hug, then thanked Sam for looking after him so well. "He's a bit young to be doing this," she said, waving goodbye. Sam wanted to thank Splodge's parents for helping him find his mum and dad, but there was no time. He was interrupted by the noise of police cars screeching down the road. Splodge just had time to wave before the doors of the spaceship closed behind him. Then there was a whirling noise and in a shower of lights and glitter they were gone.

The police were now knocking loudly on the front door. "Mr and Mrs Hardbottom," they shouted, "open up in the name of the law."

It was the best homecoming ever. Mum
and Dad were over the moon to see their
beloved boy. They couldn't have been
more proud of Sam, and how well he had
coped under such appalling circumstances.
It was hard to believe that Hilda could
have turned out to be so cruel and horrible.

It had been Maureen Cook who had
alerted the police. They had arrived just in
time to see sparks coming from behind
the garden wall.

They had driven Sam home in style to
his parents, the blue lights flashing all the
way to 2 Plunket Road.

Ernie had been taken away for questioning, while Hilda was caught trying to get on a flight for Majorca. It was her pink face with its green spots that had given her away.

Mr and Mrs Hardbottom were both charged with abduction and trying to take money under false pretences.

The Comet

The neighbour from hell

Hilda had at last found the fame she had been looking for. Her picture appeared on every newspaper, with the caption "The neighbour from hell." She was sent to prison. Ernie was let off with a caution. The judge felt that if he hadn't been so frightened of his wife he wouldn't have gone along with her plan.

Mum and Dad felt relieved that it was all over, and they were just happy to be back on earth with Sam.

The funny thing was they had no memory at all of what happened to them, except of falling asleep on the homeward journey and waking up again as they were landing. Everyone on board had been most surprised to find out that anything had been wrong, or that they had been missing for so long. Even the officials at Houston agreed that the space shuttle disappearance was a mystery.

"It's like it became invisible," said one Houston scientist.

Sam kept quiet about Splodge. Who would believe him? At her trial Hilda had gone on about aliens, and how boys couldn't be seen, only heard. Everyone thought she had gone barmy.

After it was all over, Ernie lived quietly next door, pottering in his garden. One evening while Sam was kicking a football round, Ernie leaned over the fence and said to him, "There's something that really bothers me."

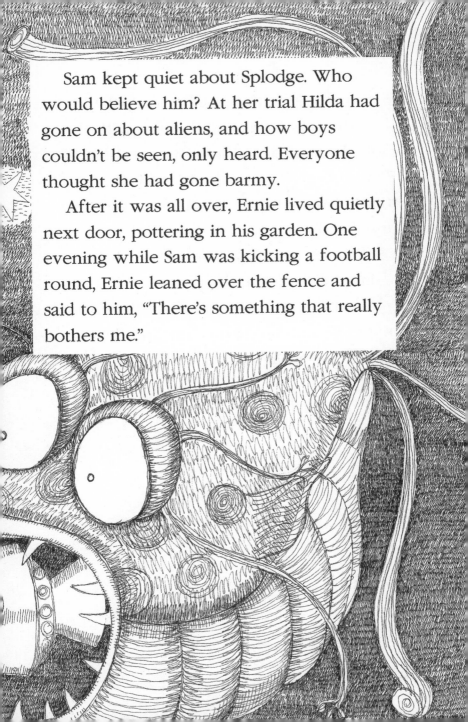

"What?" said Sam.

"That little fellow Splodge, he asked me something as I was helping him with the radio. He said did I know the meaning of 57 varieties? Do you think," said Ernie, "that he was talking about space and the universe?"

"Tomato ketchup," said Sam.

Ernie looked puzzled.

"That's what it says on the ketchup bottle, 57 varieties," said Sam, and they both burst out laughing.

More  Stories

The Strongest Girl in the World

Josie Jenkins, aged eight and three quarters, is good at doing tricks, but she amazes herself and everyone else with her strength when she lifts a table, a car, and even a bus with no effort at all. Mr Two Suit promises to bring her fame and fortune – and so he does. But when Josie and her mum and dad and brother Louis are flown to New York and she becomes a celebrity, she finds that she has to cope with all kinds of ups and downs.

The Smallest Girl Ever

Everyone expects Ruby Genie to have the same fantastic magical powers as her famous parents did. But Ruby can't do any magic at all. Or so she thinks. Then Ruby begins to get smaller... and smaller. And she discovers that even though she is so tiny she can fit into a handbag, she can still be clever and brave and find people to love her.

The Boy Who Could Fly

One day the Fat Fairy turns up at Thomas Top's house
to grant him a birthday wish. Thomas can't think what
to ask for, so he wishes he could fly. That's how Thomas
goes from being just an ordinary boy whom no one
notices to being the most popular boy in the school. But
it makes him sad that grown-ups can't see the wonderful
things he can do – especially his dad.

The Boy with the Magic Numbers

When Billy Pickles' dad leaves home to live in New
York, he gives Billy a moneybox. Billy's not sure where
to put in the money, and not sure why his dad has left.

When Billy goes to New York to visit his father and his
Italian grandmother, he discovers the secret of his magic
moneybox at last. In a wonderful adventure, he takes
Mighty Mamma on a helipcopter ride, cracks open a
safe, solves a kidnap mystery – and gets to know his
dad again.